Statistical
Applications
in Criminal
Justice

LAW AND CRIMINAL JUSTICE SERIES

Series Editor: James A. Inciardi
Division of Criminal Justice, University of Delaware

The **Law and Criminal Justice Series** provides students in criminal justice, criminology, law, sociology, and related fields with a set of short textbooks on major topics and subareas of the field. The texts range from books that introduce the basic elements of criminal justice for lower-division undergraduates to more advanced topics of current interest for advanced undergraduates and beginning graduate students. Each text is concise, didactic, and produced in an inexpensive paperback as well as hardcover format. Each author addresses the major issues and areas of current concern in that topic area, reporting on and synthesizing major research done on the subject. Case examples, chapter summaries, and discussion questions are generally included in each volume to aid in classroom use. The modular format of the series provides attractive alternatives to large, expensive classroom textbooks and timely supplements to more traditional class materials.

Volumes in this series:

Additional volumes currently in development.

Statistical Applications in Criminal Justice

Gennaro F. Vito

Edward J. Latessa

Volume 10.
Law and Criminal Justice Series

SAGE PUBLICATIONS
The Publishers of Professional Social Science
Newbury Park   London   New Delhi

10-20-95

> *We dedicate this text to our parents:*
> Rose and Ronald Vito
> Amelia and Edward Latessa

For information address:

SAGE Publications, Inc.
2111 West Hillcrest Drive
Newbury Park, California 91320

SAGE Publications Ltd.
28 Banner Street
London EC1Y 8QE
England

SAGE Publications India Pvt. Ltd.
M-32 Market
Greater Kailash I
New Delhi 110 048 India

Printed in the United States of America

Library of Congress Cataloging-in-Publication Data

Vito, Gennaro F.
    Statistical applications in criminal justice / by Gennaro F. Vito.
Edward J. Latessa.
        p.   cm.
    Bibliography: p.
    Includes index.
    ISBN 0-8039-2982-X. — ISBN 0-8039-2983-8 (pbk.)
    1. Criminal statistics.   I. Latessa, Edward J.   II. Title.
HV6018.V58   1989
364′.01′5195—dc19   88-36653
                                                                CIP

SECOND PRINTING, 1990

CONTENTS

PREFACE

This text is the result of a combined total of eighteen years of teaching basic statistics classes to undergraduate criminal justice students at both the University of Louisville and the University of Cincinnati. It is an outgrowth of a collaborative effort to develop a set of class notes designed to lead our "math-scared" charges through their paces and see the utility and value of statistical analysis. We developed this approach largely because it was the method used by our professors in the Sociology Department at Ohio State University: professors Kent Schwirian, Wen Li, and Robert Jiobu. They recognized that students who were struggling to learn statistical concepts did not need to labor over the construction of class notes as well. Over a period of years, we created sets of class notes, exchanged them as well as examinations and assignments. This basic text is the culmination of this work.

This text is designed to be "user friendly." It is written for students and has been tested in our classes. We hope that our colleagues will see the usefulness of our approach and adopt it for their classes. Otherwise, it is not written for them. The person well versed in statistics will find this text superficial and simple because it is meant to be. In fact, we do not believe that this text should be used alone. Specifically, the authors recommend its use in conjunction with Freeman F. Elzey's *A Programmed Introduction to Statistics* (Brooks/Cole, 1971) and Vito, Latessa, and Wilson, *Introduction to Criminal Justice Research Methods*(Charles C Thomas, 1988).

The one advantage this text has over the multitude of other statistics books on the market is that it offers concrete examples from criminal justice. This is another learning tool we picked up from our mentors. It is much more meaningful (and even easier) to apply statistical concepts to data and a subject matter that has specific relevance to you. Otherwise, you are likely to be overwhelmed by terms that have no meaning applied to a subject that has no bearing on your chosen career. We hope that this text serves your student audience as well as its "rough draft" predecessors have served ours, and that students will use it as a springboard to more complex analyses that we can learn from as well.

We thank Dr. Wayne Usui of the Department of Sociology at the University of Louisville for providing the tables "Areas Under the Normal Curve" and "Distribution of t," and "Critical Values for the Chi-Square Distribution." We also thank Stephen Holmes for the preparation of all figures in the text.

1

INTRODUCTION TO STATISTICS

This textbook focuses on the presentation of basic statistical concepts commonly used in criminal justice research. Specifically, it provides criminological examples to demonstrate the calculation of basic statistics in the hope that this method of presentation will give the student a firm grasp of this often frightening subject. We begin with a review of basic principles and use of the pocket calculator.

REVIEW OF BASIC MATHEMATICAL PRINCIPLES

By now, you have probably come down with a bad case of "math anxiety" or the "I can't count" blues. Unfortunately, whether we like it or not, statistics deals with numbers and their manipulation through all the usual arithmetic operations. No doubt you learned these concepts in high school, or even sooner. Naturally, you have forgotten most of them since you do not need to know them to balance your checkbook. Therefore, some review is in order. You must be able to perform some basic mathematical operations. You should relax! After all, you have several very significant "helpers" that were not available to the authors of this text when they were students—the pocket calculator and the personal computer.

It is essential that you make peace with your calculator. If you do not own one, here are some tips to guide your purchase. Buy a calculator that has a square root key and at least one memory. These features will make your calculations much easier. Some calculators are "solar powered" and eliminate the possibility that your battery will go dead during some meaningful calculation, like your examination! Once you obtain a calculator, take the time to become familiar with its operations and functions. It will do you no good if you cannot turn it on or inadvertently erase everything in the middle of a long calculation.

NOTATIONS OF ARITHMETIC OPERATIONS

Multiplication is usually indicated in the following ways:

$$2 \times 4 = 8$$
$$(2)\ (4) = 8$$

Division is usually indicated by:

$$6 \div 2 = 3$$
$$6 \ / \ 2 = 3$$

Often, statistical analysis requires that you square the number or multiply it by itself (i.e., $5^2 = 25$ or $6^2 = 36$). When you take the square root of a number, you are determining the number which, when multiplied by itself, yields the figure in question.

Order of Operations

Numbers can be added in any order:

$$4 + 2 + 6 = 12$$
$$2 + 4 + 6 = 12$$
$$4 + 6 + 2 = 12$$
$$6 + 2 + 4 = 12$$

Numbers may also be multiplied in any order:

$$12 \times 3 \times 2 = 72$$
$$2 \times 3 \times 12 = 72$$
$$3 \times 12 \times 2 = 72$$

Statistical formulas often feature several terms enclosed in parentheses, collected above or below a dividing bar or under a radical sign (square root: $\sqrt{\ }$). Therefore, you must know how to properly handle each of these conditions or you will make errors. When you encounter these conditions, the operations indicated within the parentheses must be performed *first*.

$$3(8 - 2) = 3(6) = 18$$

To make matters more complicated, statistical formulas also present "nested" parentheses. When this happens, remember the "breakout rule"— perform the operations within the innermost parentheses *first*. In other words, you "break out" of the parentheses from the inside out.

$$4[2 + 6(12 - 3) - 7(3 + 2)] =$$
$$4[2 + 6(9) - 7(5)] =$$
$$4[2 + 54 - 35] =$$
$$4[2 + 19] = 4[21] = 84$$

You must also remember that when parentheses are not present to guide your operations, multiplication and division are performed *before* addition and subtraction.

$$3 \times 2 + 3 + 8 \div 2 = 13$$

First, multiply 3 times 2 to obtain 6. Then, divide 8 by 2 to obtain 4. So, $6 + 3 + 4 = 13$.

SIGNED NUMBERS

Statistical formulas commonly feature signed numbers, positive (zero or greater) and negative (less than zero). Unless a negative sign is present, assume that the number is positive. There are specific rules to follow when you manipulate signed numbers.

Addition

(1) To add numbers of the same sign, add the digits and assign the common sign to the sum.

$$(-6) + (-9) + (-2) = -17$$
$$(2) + (9) + (6) = 17$$

(2) When adding two numbers which do not have the same signs, subtract the smaller from the larger and assign the sign of the larger number to the answer.

$$(-8) + (+5) = -3$$
$$(+6) + (-1) = 5$$

(3) When adding more than two numbers of unlike signs, add the positive numbers and negative numbers separately, then subtract the smaller figure from the larger figure. Finally, assign the sign of the larger figure to the answer.

$$(+5) + (-3) + (-2) + (+7)$$

becomes

$$(+5) + (+7) = 12 \text{ and } (-3) + (-2) = -5$$

or

$$12 + (-5) = 7$$

Subtraction

(1) To subtract one signed number from another, change the sign of the number to be subtracted and proceed as if you were adding the numbers.

$$
\begin{aligned}
(+7) - (+5) &= 7 - 5 = 2 \\
(+4) - (-3) &= 4 + 3 = 7 \\
(-9) - (-2) &= -9 + 2 = -7 \\
(-6) - (+3) &= -6 - 3 = -9
\end{aligned}
$$

Multiplication

(1) When you multiply two numbers of the same sign, the product is *always* positive.

$$
\begin{aligned}
(+3)(+8) &= 24 \\
(-3)(-8) &= 24
\end{aligned}
$$

(2) When you multiply two numbers of different signs, the product is *always* negative.

$$
\begin{aligned}
(+2)(-8) &= -16 \\
(-2)(+7) &= -14
\end{aligned}
$$

Division

(1) When you divide two numbers of the same sign, the quotient is *always* positive.

$$
\begin{aligned}
(+45) \div (+5) &= 9 \\
(-16) \div (-2) &= 8
\end{aligned}
$$

(2) When you divide two numbers of different signs, the quotient is *always* negative.

$$(+12) \div (-4) = -3$$
$$(-45) \div (+5) = -9$$

Again, you have met these rules in your previous life as high school students. You now must become reacquainted with them to avoid errors in your statistical calculations. Review these concepts until they become "second nature" once again.

ROUNDING NUMBERS

In statistical analysis, numbers are often expressed in decimal form. However, you must follow some form of convention to determine how many figures to use when computing and eventually reporting results. We will use the following conventions in this textbook, (1) until we obtain the final answer, we will keep as many digits as we comfortably can (in our calculator), and (2) we will round all final answers to the nearest tenth.

The following "conventions" are typically observed when rounding numbers. If the first of the digits to be dropped is less than five (< 5), drop them with no change in the preceeding number (i.e., $43.42 = 43.4$). If the digit(s) to be dropped are greater than five (> 5), raise the preceeding number by one (i.e., $43.46 = 43.5$). Again, these rules are easy to follow and will not drastically affect the accuracy of your calculations.

CALCULATING PERCENTAGE TRENDS

Another very common illustration used in statistical presentations is percentage trends. We are often concerned with presenting information about the trends in crime rates over time. This is a simple concept but it is often miscalculated.

The following example is taken directly from the 1985 *Uniform Crime Reports* for the crimes of murder and nonnegligent manslaughter:

TREND

Year	Number of Offenses
1984	18,692
1985	18,976

The percentage trend reported is $+1.5$ percent. How was this trend calculated? The base year is 1984, and the denominator in our equation. First, subtract the two figures to determine the difference in the number of reported murders ($18,976 - 18,692 = 284$). Since the total number of murders reported in 1985 was greater than that of 1984, 284 represents an increase in reported homicides. Finally, we divide 284 by 18,692 to determine the percentage trend—an increase of 1.5% in the number of reported murders.

Mastery of these basic mathematical principles should alleviate your "math anxiety" and allow you to concentrate on the interpretation of statistical results rather than on the calculation of the "right" answer.

THE MAJOR PURPOSES OF STATISTICAL ANALYSIS

Statistics are a set of tools that students can use to make decisions based on limited information. These methods help researchers deal with numbers effectively, organize them, and extract useful information. Typically, in criminal justice research, statistical analysis allows the researcher to make some determination about a theory or a treatment, or evaluate the performance of a program or a law. Statistics also help summarize information. They can tell the researcher how seriously to regard apparent differences between the results of programs and treatments and to determine the extent of a relationship between sets of data.

For example, legislators in Kentucky recently wrestled with ways to reduce the size of the prison population. One proposal was to change the dollar value of property stolen in larceny felonies. At that time, Theft by Unlawful Taking (TBUT) was a felony if the property was valued at fifty dollars or more. This sounds like a logical proposition, but what information would we want to know before we implemented such a change? This is where statistics can enter into the decision-making process, providing information. A study of Kentucky felony case processing (Vito and Ellis, 1985) revealed that, for every 100 TBUT arrests, only eight offenders were sentenced to state prisons. These data reveal that a change in the dollar amount would affect only a small number of the individuals entering prison. Consideration of such a report could lead the legislators to look elsewhere for ways to reduce the prison population.

BASIC DEFINITIONS

Here are some general definitions that we will meet in our review of statistics. Learning these concepts is like learning a foreign language— "statisticese." However, there is one crucial difference, statistical terms are very literal and describe the concept under consideration in a straightforward manner. If you will think about what the term means (in regular English), you will be able to master "statisticese" with less difficulty. For example, descriptive statistics are statistics that *describe* or summarize the characteristics of a set of data. Inferential statistics move beyond the description of the characteristics of your set of data to make *inferences* about the larger population from which your sample was drawn. A population is the larger grouping of elements under consideration. Due to limitations of time and money, researchers typically select a sample to stand in place of the population. For example, you may draw a sample of juvenile delinquents and conduct a survey rather than attempt to contact every juvenile delinquent in the state. The sample is representative of the population if all members of the population have an equal chance of being selected in the sample (random selection).

We will also spend some time talking about different types of hypotheses and variables. A hypothesis is a statement about what is present in the real world if the theory is true. For example, if deterrence works, the homicide rate should fall in the period following the execution of a convicted murderer.

A variable is an attribute you are measuring that usually has more than one possible value. Variables have an operational definition, which specifically states the concrete and specific way in which the variable is measured. An operational definition of recidivism could be, "reincarceration in a state prison." A dependent variable is one that depends upon, or is influenced by, another variable. An independent variable influences or produces an effect upon a dependent variable. For example, prior record (independent) affects the probability of recidivism (dependent variable). These introductory definitions provide a backdrop for the more detailed information which will follow. Now, let us turn to another key concept in statistical analysis, levels of measurement.

LEVELS OF MEASUREMENT

Levels of measurement relate to how the variables used in an analysis are scaled. Often, we assign numbers to variables in order to make them more amenable to statistical analysis. The level of measurement specifically refers to the relationship between the variables (your observations) and the numbers assigned to them. The concept is extremely significant because the type of statistical analysis permissible on a set of data is dependent upon the level of measurement. As such, the level of measurement is usually one of the foremost assumptions behind the use of a certain statistical test. As we shall see, most statistical tests rest upon certain fundamental assumptions which, if violated, can make the results useless or inconsequential.

Here, a rather simple test is available. When examining a variable to determine the level of measurement, simply ask yourself the question, "Are the numbers used to represent each variable serving as numbers (which can be added, subtracted, multiplied and divided) or as codes or symbols?" Note that the level of measurement is only an issue when you have assigned numbers to the variables. When you are actually counting something, like the number of burglaries reported to the police last year, the concept does not apply. In this case, you would analyze an actual number (again, burglaries reported) and would not be assigning numbers to a certain observation. This distinction should become more apparent as we move through the various levels of measurement (Siegel).

Nominal Scale

The nominal scale is measurement at its lowest level. Here, numbers classify the characteristics of the variable under consideration. An example of a nominal scale is one in which numbers identify the groups to which various objects belong. If we classified racial groups as (1) black, or (2) white and then applied it to Sam (white) and Joe (black), the only inference we could draw is that Sam and Joe are from different racial groups. We could not arrange the groups in any meaningful order nor could we calculate distances between racial groups. Another example of a nominal scale is when numbers attached to categories serve as substitutes for names (i.e., arrest numbers given to defendants at booking). In this manner, the nominal scale classifies the attributes of a variable. A nominal scale also has the property of equivalence: the members of any one subclass are the same. Persons or items cannot belong to more than one category. The nominal scale tells us that the values we have observed either belong to either the same or different categories.

Ordinal Scale

An ordinal scale has all of the characteristics of a nominal scale. It also introduces the concept of ranking. Now, the items on the scale not only differ from one another, but they also stand in relation to one another. Specifically, some items on the scale are "greater than" ($>$) others in the variable under consideration. Let us take several of the "Index Crimes" from the *Uniform Crime Reports* as an example of an ordinal scale. The Federal Bureau of Investigation annually reports the crimes reported to the police in the United States. A central feature of this report is the Index Crime Scale. The crimes are ranked by their severity as indicators of the extent of the crime problem. Assigning numbers, our new Crime Index consists of:

(1) Murder
(2) Forcible Rape
(3) Robbery
(4) Aggravated Assault
(5) Burglary
(6) Motor Vehicle Theft
(7) Larceny-Theft

This index represents the attributes of an ordinal scale. Let us take (1) murder and (3) robbery as examples. Using the index as a basis, what conclusions can we reach about these two crimes? First, murder and robbery have different ranks and are different crimes. This is the attribute of equivalence and means that the index is at least a nominal scale. Second, a murder (ranked first) is worse than a robbery (ranked third). However, we cannot reach any meaningful conclusions about the distance between murder and robbery on the index. Murder and robbery are simply one "category" or "rank" apart.

Again, the ordinal scale introduces the attribute of ranking or ordering items on a scale. Like a nominal scale, it has the property of equivalence. It also introduces the concept of transitivity: If A exceeds B and B exceeds C, then A *must* exceed C. In our Crime Index example, transitivity means that if murder is considered more severe than rape and rape is more severe than robbery, then murder *must* be more severe than robbery.

Interval Scale

This type of scale has all of the characteristics of an ordinal scale. In addition, the distance between any two numbers (the interval) on the scale is of a known size. The interval scale features a common and constant unit of measurement which assigns a real number to all pairs of objects in the scale. A common interval scale is time. For example, a burglary is reported to the police at 7:00 P.M. and a murder is reported at 9:00 P.M. Here, we can conclude that the crimes were reported at different times (nominal scale), the murder was reported later than the burglary (ordinal scale), and that the murder was reported two hours later than the burglary (interval scale). We can say something about the size of the difference between each category. We still cannot say that the murder is 1/12 greater than the burglary. Yet, the interval scale allows us to count the interval, or distance, between observations. We are now able to perform arithmetic operations on such a variable.

Ratio Scale

The ratio scale is the strongest level of measurement. It has all of the attributes of an interval scale plus a true zero point as its origin. The zero point permits us to calculate and state the ratio between any two values on the scale. A good example is age. Sam is 30 and Joe is 15. Here, we can conclude that Joe and Sam have different ages (nominal scale), Sam is older than Joe (ordinal), Joe is fifteen years younger than Sam (interval scale), and Sam is *twice* as old as Joe—the ratio of their ages is two to one.

We shall see that, at a given level of measurement, only certain statistical operations are possible. Again, the differences typically relate to the extent to which the numbers on your scale (which represent the variable in question) are functioning as true numbers or as codes. Table 1.1 summarizes the properties of the different levels of measurement.

TABLE 1.1.   Summary Scale: Attributes of Levels of Measurement

	Level			
	Nominal	*Ordinal*	*Interval*	*Ratio*
Property				
1. Classification	Yes	Yes	Yes	Yes
2. Ranking	No	Yes	Yes	Yes
3. Distance	No	No	Yes	Yes
4. Zero Point	No	No	No	Yes

SUMMARY

In this chapter, we reviewed some fundamental principles of arithmetic and introduced some basic statistical concepts. When studying statistics, it is important to remember that the concepts and ideas build upon each other and accumulate. For example, the attributes of the levels of measurement carried over from one level to another. Each level possesses all of the attributes of the previous level, plus one new attribute. Therefore, it is very important to learn these concepts as presented since you will continue to use them throughout the course. Again, the levels of measurement principle will serve as the basis for which statistical tests are permitted on a given set of data.

EXERCISES

Perform the following operations:

1. Addition

$$\begin{array}{rrrrrrrrrr} 8 & 4 & 8 & 30 & 10 & -6 & -6 & -9 & -7 & -16 \\ -3 & -2 & -9 & -10 & -6 & 2 & 3 & 1 & -6 & 0 \end{array}$$

2. Subtraction

$$\begin{array}{rrrrrrrrr} -8 & 4 & 8 & 20 & -6 & -9 & 0 & -4 & -10 \\ -3 & -2 & -9 & -10 & 3 & 1 & -16 & -2 & -10 \end{array}$$

3. $(49 + 8) \div 7 =$

4. $(6 \times 2 \times 2) \div 2 =$
5. $(.25)(4 \times 6) =$
6. $(4 + 2) \div 4 =$
7. $2(2 \times 5) \div 1 =$
8. $(6 \times 5) \div (2 \times 3) =$
9. $(2 / 6) \div (1 / 3) =$
10. $(6 + 1)^2$
11. $(.04 / .02) =$
12. $(4 + 1)^2$
13. $(2 + 3)^2$
14. $(.04 / .002) =$
15. $(-.04) / (.02) =$
16. $(-150) (0) =$
17. $(-3)(2) =$
18. $(2)(-5) =$
19. $(-1)(-6) =$
20. $(-1)(0) =$
21. $4^2 + 1^2 + 3^2 + 9^2 =$
22. $(-7)(-8)(-1)(-1) =$
23.   11523.33
     6790.02
     4838.91
       10.53
      999.18
 -15730.00

24. Using our conventions, round the following numbers to the nearest tenth:
   3.265
  41.522
322.315
 47.552
 52.550
 52.651
 52.650

25. The following figures represent the number of homicides reported to Los Angeles Police Precincts during the past two years (January–June):

Precinct	1988	1987
Central	13	19
Hollenbeck	17	22
Newton	38	45
Northeast	10	21
Rampart	22	39

Harbor	20	9
Southwest	24	39
77th	50	77
Southeast	41	54
Hollywood	11	22
Pacific	11	4
West L.A.	11	7
Wilshire	13	23
Devonshire	9	4
Foothill	17	14
N. Hollywood	7	5
Van Nuys	10	6
West Valley	6	6

Calculate the percentage trend for this distribution. First, calculate the total trend between 1987 and 1988, then calculate the trend between 1987 and 1988 precinct by precinct. What is the pattern?

KEY TERMS

descriptive statistics

inferential statistics

population

hypothesis

variable

operational definition

dependent variable

independent variable

levels of measurement

nominal scale

equivalence

ordinal scale

index crimes

transitivity

interval scale

ratio scale

REFERENCES

SIEGEL, S. (1956) *Nonparametric statistics for the behavioral sciences.* New York: McGraw-Hill.

VITO, G. F., and J. B. ELLIS (1985) *An offender based tracking system study of three judicial districts in the Commonwealth of Kentucky.* Louisville: University of Louisville, Kentucky Criminal Justice Statistical Analysis Center.

2

BASIC DESCRIPTIVE STATISTICS

In this chapter, we will begin to calculate and interpret statistics. Our objective is to describe the data we have collected and analyze it in a manner easily understood by our audience. Basically, we will be using one of the major functions of statistics—data reduction. Through the use of some "summary" statistical measures we can communicate information that describes the characteristics of the sample under consideration.

CONSTRUCTING A FREQUENCY DISTRIBUTION

The first step in many analyses is to construct a frequency distribution, a distribution of scores which lists the number (frequency) of scores for each value. It serves as a basis for statistical analysis and for the graphic presentation of that data. A basic description of the data set is the first step in any statistical analysis. For example, we have collected data on the number of previous convictions for a group of repeat offenders, and are interested in the number of prior convictions (X) for this group. How many of them have three prior convictions, or what is the highest number of prior convictions? It is necessary to construct a frequency distribution to answer these questions.

Prior Convictions of Repeat Offenders

X (Score)	f (Frequency)	fX
8	3	24
7	5	35
6	6	36
5	8	40
4	2	8
3	6	18
2	8	16
1	9	9
	$N = 47$	$\Sigma fX = 186$

The X (or score) column of this distribution tells us that our sample of 47 repeat offenders (N) have between one and eight prior convictions. Three inmates had eight prior convictions, five had seven, seven had six and so on. All together, they accounted for a total of 186 convictions (ΣfX).

This example reveals that the first thing you do when constructing a frequency distribution is to establish an array, a set of numerical values arranged in order from the highest to the lowest score magnitude. The array is listed in the X column. The f (or frequency) column tells us how many times that particular score occurred in the distribution. The fX column indicates the total number of score values. For example, line one indicates that three offenders had eight prior convictions for a total of twenty-four prior convictions.

The first summary statistic we will consider is the range. The range of a distribution is the highest score minus the lowest score (H − L). So, for the above distribution, the range is: $8 - 1 = 7$. The range gives us a limited amount of information but it is quite useful when a researcher wishes to condense a frequency distribution. This is called grouping the data into classes. In order to group data, a class interval (i) is used:

$$\text{Class Interval } (i) = \frac{\text{Range}}{N \text{ of cases desired by researcher}}$$

So, for our conviction data:

$$i = \frac{8 - 1}{4} = \frac{7}{4} = 1.75; \text{ round to } 2.$$

Grouping our conviction data, the new distribution would be:

Interval	f
8–7	8
6–5	14
4–3	8
2–1	17
	$N = 47$

Here, we can see that the distribution changes somewhat because we have grouped the data. But the nature of the data remains the same.

Another concept must be introduced here. Statistical formulas (i.e., the median) ask for the lower limit of a number (ll). To determine the lower limit of a number, subtract 0.5. To determine the upper limit of a number, add 0.5. Therefore, the lower limit of 10 is 9.5 and the upper limit of 10 is 10.5.

Frequency distributions also serve as the basis for the graphic presentation of data, which we will consider later in this chapter.

DESCRIPTIVE STATISTICS

Whether we are aware of it or not, we are all familiar with descriptive statistics. We encounter them constantly in everyday life. Descriptive statistics are techniques used to organize and make data understandable. They enable the researcher to describe the characteristics of a sample, to deal with great quantities of data, and to arrange it so it is easier to comprehend.

The most common forms of descriptive statistics are called *measures of central tendency*. They provide a concise description of the average, or most typical value present in a distribution of scores. These measures of central tendency are the mode, the median, and the mean.

The Mode

The mode is the number that occurs more frequently than any other in a distribution. The mode requires no statistical computation or formula since you can observe it directly by reading the frequency distribution. Let us examine data compiled from a substance abuse program evaluation.

X (Reported Substance Abuse)	f
Alcohol	85
Drugs	32
Cross Addicted	62

Here, we see that most of the clients of this program (85) were alcoholics. In the next example, we see that a distribution can have more than one mode.

X (Program Client Status)	f
Completed Supervision	25
Prison	10
Still Under Supervision	25

This is an example of a bimodal distribution. The program had twenty-five clients who completed their period of supervision and another twenty-five still under supervision. If there are more than two scores that are the same, the distribution is said to be multimodal. The mode can be found at any level of measurement. It is the point at which the scores are most densely concentrated. It can rest at the extreme end of a distribution but it is completely unaffected by extreme scores in the distribution.

The major disadvantage of the mode is that it is not subject to further statistical analysis. It does not make sense to compare modes taken from two different samples because the mode simply indicates which score was most typical in a distribution.

The Median

The second measure of central tendency is the median. It is the midpoint or middle of a distribution. It is the point at which 50% of the scores lie above and 50% lie below. It divides the distribution into equal halves (the 50th percentile). Because it is the "position average," a distribution has one and only one median. It requires an ordinal level of measurement (ranking) or higher. It is very stable, that is, it is least affected by extreme scores. Extreme scores can occur at either end of a distribution but have little or no effect on the median.

Number of Crimes Committed Since Last Arrest

X	f	f_b	fX
24	1	20	24
22	1	19	22
21	1	18	21
18	1	17	18
16	1	16	16
10	1	15	10
9	3	14	27
8	2	11	16
7	3	9	21
6	2	6	12
5	1	4	5
4	2	3	8
2	1	1	2
	$N = 20$		$\Sigma fX = 202$

The formula for computing the median is:

$$Mdn = ll + \left(\frac{.5N - \Sigma f_b}{f_w} \right) i$$

where: Σ = the sum of
          ll = the lower real limit of the interval *containing* the
                 median
          Σf_b = frequencies of the interval *below* the median
          f_w = frequencies of the interval *containing* the median
          i = the interval size in the distribution

To compute the median:

(1) It is necessary to estimate which interval contains the median. $.5N$ tells us to go halfway up from the bottom of the distribution to estimate the position of the median (from the lowest score to the highest score).

(2) Find the ll (or the lower limit) of the interval containing the median.

(3) Find the Σf_b or the number of cases that occur in the distribution *before* the interval containing the $.5N$ score.

(4) Find f_w, or the number of cases in the interval containing the $.5N$ score.

(5) Find i or the interval size in the distribution. Note that with ungrouped data, this value will equal one, but with grouped data, it will vary according to the number of scores in the interval. For example, for the interval $1 - 3$, $i = .3$.

(6) Put all this together into the formula and solve.

$$Mdn = ll + \left(\frac{.5N - \Sigma f_b}{f_w} \right) i$$

$$7.5 + \left(\frac{.5(20) - 9}{2} \right) 1$$

$$7.5 + 0.5 = 8$$

$$Mdn = 8$$

The Mean

The final measure of central tendency we will examine is the mean $(\overline{X})$. The mean is the average score in the distribution. It is the value obtained by adding the scores in a set of data and then dividing this sum by the total number of scores.

$$Mean\ (\overline{X}) = \frac{\Sigma fX}{N}$$

Using the data from our "Crimes Committed Since Last Arrest" example:

$$\text{Mean } (\overline{X}) = \frac{\Sigma fX}{N}$$

$$\overline{X} = \frac{202}{20} = 10.1$$

A distribution can have one and only one mean. It is the most popular and frequently used measure of central tendency. Unlike the mode and median, it is open to further statistical analysis and comparison between samples or subgroups. The mean converts the sum of scores into an amount per element, giving a measure that you can compare across different groups. For example, you can compare the average (mean) rate of burglaries from cities of different sizes because the size of the city has been converted so that the largest city will not automatically have the highest mean burglary rate.

One of the characteristics of the mean is that the sum of the deviations (x) from the mean *always* equals zero. Consider the following example:

X	f	fX	$x = (X - \overline{X})$
5	1	5	2
4	1	4	1
3	1	3	0
2	1	2	−1
1	1	1	−2
	$N = 5$	$\Sigma fX = 15$	0

$$\text{Mean } (\overline{X}) = \frac{\Sigma fX}{N}$$

$$\overline{X} = \frac{15}{5} = 3$$

One of the disadvantages of the mean is that it is affected by extreme scores in a distribution. For example, the following are ages of persons arrested for armed robbery:

25   26   27   30   31   32   33   76   32

The mean age is 34, but seven of the arrestees are under 33. The elderly 76-year-old armed robber is pulling up the value of the mean. Therefore, a change in any one score in a distribution will change the value of the mean of that distribution.

The mean is appropriate for use with interval or ratio level data because it makes use of information about the distance between each item on the measurement scale. The mean is also the appropriate measure to use when making an inference from a sample to a population. Remember, a population is a complete set of individuals (i.e., all the members of a police department). Typically, due to limitations of time and money, researchers will examine the attributes of a sample of the population which is drawn in such a way that it is representative of the population. Then, the researcher can make inferences about the population based upon the data collected and analyzed from the sample.

The mean is more stable than the median when making statistical inferences. If a large number of samples were drawn from the same population, the mean varies less than the median from sample to sample. Thus, the mean should be employed to measure the central tendency of a distribution whenever a researcher wants to study a sample for the purpose of estimating the value of the population mean.

When you are describing a sample and writing a report, it is appropriate to report all the measures of central tendency. In the example, the "Number of Crimes Committed by a Sample of Probationers Since Their Last Arrest," the mode = 7, 9; the median = 8; and the mean = 10.1.

Descriptive statistics are important because they give a clearer picture of the major characteristics of a set of numbers. They help to communicate information to decision makers in an efficient manner. Percentiles are another useful statistical tool which help to describe a set of numbers.

PERCENTILES

Percentiles tell us how scores stand in relation to one another. A percentile is a measure used to indicate the relative position of a score within a frequency distribution. The percentile of a score indicates the percent of the total number of cases that fall below the score under consideration. For example, if a score of 39 is the tenth percentile, 10% of the total number of cases scored below 39. Percentiles are often grouped into deciles and quartiles. One percentile equals one percent, a decile refers to 10 percentage points and a quartile 25 percentage points in a distribution. D_1 is the first decile and 10% of the scores in the distribution fall below it. Q_1 is the first quartile and 25% of the scores in the distribution are below it.

To calculate the percentiles we perform the following operations, which should be familiar to us. After all, the median is the 50th percentile so we have already used this formula!

Reported Burglaries in City Police Districts (June)

X (Number of Burglaries)	f (Number of Districts)
39	1
35	4
30	3
27	7
25	5
21	9
18	15
	N = 44

Let us determine the number of burglaries associated with the 60th percentile. First, we must estimate the point at which the 60th percentile lies. To make this determination, we multiply the N by .60 (the value of the percentile we are seeking).

$$44 \times .6 = 26.4$$

Now we count from the bottom of the distribution until we find the score that lies 26.4 units from the bottom. We had 15 districts with 18 burglaries, 9 districts with 21 burglaries and 5 districts with 25 burglaries. $15 + 9 + 5 = 29$, so we estimate that the 60th percentile corresponds with the score of 25 burglaries. Next, we plug this value into the following formula (again, note that this formula is just a variation of the formula used to calculate the median).

$$\text{60th percentile} = ll + \left(\frac{.6N - \Sigma f_b}{f_w} \right) i$$

$$\text{60th percentile} = 24.5 + \left(\frac{26.4 - 24}{5} \right) 1$$

$$\text{60th percentile} = 24.5 + 0.48 = 24.98 \text{ or } 25$$

ll = lower limit of the score
Σf_b = the sum of the frequencies below the category that contains the score
f_w = frequency within the category that contains the score
i = the interval size in the distribution

Thus, we can say that 60% of the police districts reported less than 25 burglaries during the month of June.

Using grouped data, the calculation of the percentile follows the same format.

Time Served by 72 Parolees from San Quentin

X (Years)	f (Number of Parolees)
28–30	1
25–27	4
22–24	2
19–21	3
16–18	4
13–15	9
10–12	14
7–9	20
4–6	10
1–3	5
	N = 72

To answer the question, "How many years did it take 40% of the inmates to make parole?" we would calculate the value of the 40th percentile.

$$\text{40th percentile} = ll + \left(\frac{.4N - \Sigma f_b}{f_w} \right) i$$

$$\text{40th percentile} = ll + \left(\frac{.4(72) - 15}{20} \right) 3$$

$$\text{40th percentile} = 6.5 + \left(\frac{28.8 - 15}{20} \right) 3$$

$$\text{40th percentile} = 6.5 + \left(\frac{13.8}{20} \right) 3$$

$$\text{40th percentile} = 6.5 + (.69) 3$$

$$\text{40th percentile} = 6.5 + 2.1 = 8.6$$

Therefore, 40% of the 72 inmates from San Quentin were released on parole after serving, at most, 8.6 years.

MEASURES OF VARIABILITY

Now that we have reviewed some descriptive statistics, you should realize that variation is the foundation of all statistics. After all, if all the values in a given set were identical, then any single score would represent all scores, and any statistic would be meaningless. Thus, the amount of dispersion in the data is highly relevant. To measure variation we usually consider either (1) measurements of range that include all or a specified percentage of items, or (2) averages based upon deviation of the variates from a selected value, usually the mean. Here, we will consider several measures of variability, beginning with the range.

The Range

The range is the simplest and crudest measure of variation. Since computation of the range is based upon only the two extreme values of a distribution (the highest score − the lowest score), it reveals nothing about the other scores in the distribution. For this reason, the range is affected by both the size and presence of extreme scores; it is not a stable measure. The range also assumes that the data are measured at the interval level. As demonstrated earlier, the range helps the researcher determine the number of intervals to employ in the construction of a grouped frequency distribution.

VARIANCE

The variance is the mean of the sum of all squared deviations from the mean of any distribution of scores. It is an important statistic since it summarizes the amount of dispersion, or variance, of the scores around the mean. The steps to calculate the variance are as follows:

(1) Find the mean of the distribution.
(2) Find the deviation from the mean ($x = X - \overline{X}$) for each score.
(3) Square each x to obtain x^2.
(4) Find the mean of the squared deviations. This gives you the average squared deviation from the mean or the variance.

(5) $s'^2 = \dfrac{\Sigma f x^2}{N}$

STANDARD DEVIATION

The standard deviation is the square root of the variance. It is the single number that is representative of the deviations from the mean found in that distribution. A standard deviation tells you what kind of deviation from the mean is typical of a given population. For most populations you encounter, about two-thirds of all the numbers in the population are within one standard deviation of the mean. These properties will become more evident when we examine standard scores and the normal distribution.

Number of Prior Felony Convictions Among Homicide Defendents

X	f	fX	$x = (X - \overline{X})$	x^2	fx^2
6	3	18	1.9	3.61	10.83
5	8	40	0.9	0.81	6.48
4	6	24	−0.1	0.01	0.06
3	4	12	−1.1	1.21	4.84
2	2	4	−2.1	4.41	8.82
1	1	1	−3.1	9.61	9.61
	$N = 24$	$\Sigma fX = 99$			40.64

$$\overline{X} = \frac{\Sigma fX}{N} = \frac{99}{24} = 4.1 \qquad s'^2 = \frac{\Sigma fx^2}{N} = \frac{40.64}{24} = 1.69$$

$$s' = \sqrt{s'^2} = \sqrt{1.69} = 1.3$$

In this distribution, the variance is 1.69 and the standard deviation is 1.3. We shall now see how this fits into the larger picture of the normal distribution.

THE NORMAL DISTRIBUTION

Statistics and parameters are two terms that we will encounter and it is important that you not become confused about their meanings. A parameter is a measurement of an entire population, while a statistic is a measurement of a sample. For parameters Greek letters are utilized as symbols, while statistics use Roman letters.

Measurement	Population (Parameter)	Sample (Statistics)
Mean	μ	$\overline{X}$
Variance	σ^2	s'^2
Standard Deviation	σ	s'

A normal curve refers to a certain type of distribution of scores. The

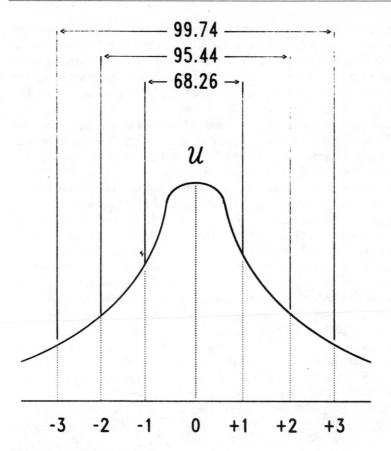

Figure 2.1. Normal Distribution

word "normal" refers to the type of curve and distribution having certain properties. The standard formula (don't panic, it is just an informative example) for a normal curve is:

$$Y = \left(\frac{1}{S\sqrt{2\pi}}\right) \quad e - \frac{1}{2}\left(\frac{X - \mu}{\sigma}\right)^2$$

Where Y is the height of the curve for any given value of X, $e = 2.72$, and pi $= 3.14$ (constants). Therefore, the formula involves only two summarizing measures, the mean and the standard deviation. Thus, the exact form of the normal curve will be known if we are given the values of both the mean and the standard deviation.

Not all symmetrical bell-shaped curves are normal curves. They can differ with respect to their peakedness due to differences in their standard deviation. One of the more desirable properties of the normal curve is that it can be used to define a series of constant attributes. The total area under the normal curve can represent the total number of units in a population. Due to this property, it is possible to determine the proportion of frequencies contained between any two scores along the x-axis by determining the area under the curve between the two scores. The normal curve can thus serve as an instrument to standardize scores taken from different distributions. It has a general comparative function.

Skewness occurs when one of the tails of the distribution is elongated, so that the distribution is asymetric. You describe skewness by measuring its degree and reporting its direction—where the elongated tail is located. In the first example we see a positive skew, with the tail to the left; the second example is negative skew, with the tail to the right.

A normal curve is always symmetrical and bell shaped. It is asymptotic, which means that the ends of the distribution extend toward infinity, approaching the horizontal axis but never quite touching it. The range of the normal distribution is theoretically infinite. The mean, median, and mode all occur at the same point, dividing the distribution into two equal parts. As displayed above, the distance in standard deviation units may be converted into a percentage of the total area. Because of its symmetry, approximately two-thirds (68.26%) of the cases lie in the interval extending + or − one standard deviation unit above and below the mean. Similarly, approximately 95% of the cases fall within + or − two standard deviation units on either side of the mean. Finally, the mean of the normal distribution is always defined as zero and the standard deviation is always equal to one. This provides a common standard to compare scores taken from different distributions.

STANDARD SCORES (Z SCORES)

Standard scores, also called Z scores, play an important role in the normal curve. Z scores are those scores taken on some characteristic from two different populations or elements that are not directly comparable. The solution to this problem of comparability lies in converting the raw measures into standardized units of measurement which are comparable. Standard scores are expressed as raw deviations from the mean as multiples of the standard deviation.

$$Z = \frac{X - \overline{X}}{s'} \quad \text{or} \quad \frac{x}{s'}$$

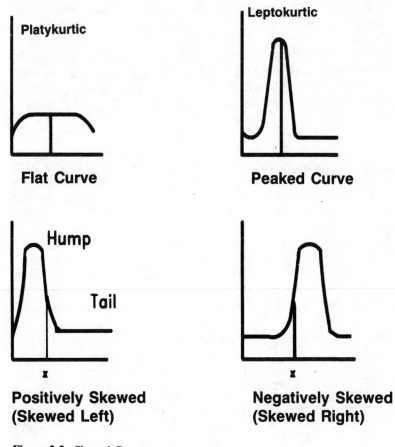

Figure 2.2. Skewed Curves

where

X is a raw score
$\overline{X}$ is the sample mean
s' is the standard deviation
x is the deviation score

Since standard scores are expressed in terms of standard deviation units, every raw score can be given an equivalent standard score. Z scores can be positive or negative depending upon which side of the mean a particular score is located. Positive Z scores fall above the mean, negative Z scores fall below the mean. The distance between any Z score and the mean of the distribution includes a corresponding proportion of the distribution. (See Figure 2.1.) Thus, the percentage of scores lying between the mean and a Z score of 1.78 is 46.25% (see Table A: "Areas Under the Normal Curve"). Remember, the sign of the Z score ($+$ or $-$) simply tells us whether or not a score is above or below the mean. The proportionate area is still the same, regardless of the sign. For example, Jerry and Ed are convicted of burglary. Ed is sentenced in Cincinnati, Jerry in Louisville.

	Jerry	Ed
Sentence	5	7
Mean Sentence for Burglary	3	5
Standard Deviation	2.3	4.1

$$Z = \frac{X - \overline{X}}{s'}$$

$$\text{Jerry} = \frac{5 - 3}{2.3} = \frac{2}{2.3} = .87$$

$$\text{Ed} = \frac{7 - 5}{4.1} = \frac{2}{4.1} = .49$$

Examining the Z scores, it is apparent that Ed received a longer sentence than burglars sentenced in Cincinnati and the same is true of Jerry in Louisville. Since so many other variables enter the sentencing process (like whether or not the judge had a fight with his girlfriend), it is difficult to say that Jerry was sentenced more harshly than Ed. It is better to compare the sentences within the respective courts than to compare them to each other. Since the area under the normal curve contains 100% of the cases, we can determine the percentage of burglars in each court whose sentences lie above and below Jerry and Ed's. Jerry's Z score was 0.87. From the Table A ("Areas Under the Normal Curve"), we see that this includes .3078 of the distribution above the mean. Since .50 cases lie below the mean, we add .3078 + .5000, or 80.7% of the Louisville burglars were sentenced to less years than Jerry. Given Ed's Z score (.49), the percentage of burglars in Cincinnati that received sentences lower than Ed's was .1879 + .50 = .6879 or 69%.

The primary advantage of standard scores is that they may be used to compare raw scores taken from different distributions (relatively, not directly). Z scores require an interval level of measurement. The primary disadvantage of Z scores is that a normal distribution must be assumed. When the distribution is skewed, the areas under the curve are not proportional. The normal curve is therefore used as a device to compare scores taken from different distributions.

SUMMARY

In this chapter, we reviewed the basic descriptive statistics that are commonly and typically used in research studies. These statistics derive information which serves as a shorthand, or summary, to describe the distribution. Thus, they make the data understandable and make it possible for the researcher to summarize the findings in reasonable and clear terminology. We also discovered the normal distribution and its characteristics. The normal curve can be used as a common measuring device to compare scores taken from a particular study or report.

EXERCISES

1. The counties in your state ($N = 90$) have reported the number of juveniles held in detention over the past year. Complete the following frequency distribution for these data and compute the mode, mean, median, variance, and standard deviation.

X	f
49	5
38	8
36	12
32	15
29	6
21	15
19	20
11	1
8	5
1	3

2. Using the following data on Kentucky executions, construct an ungrouped frequency distribution, calculate the mean, median, standard deviation, and variance. What was the modal year (in the list below)?

Persons Executed in the Commonwealth of Kentucky, 1911-1962
Methods: Hanging and Electrocution

1911:	4	1927:	1	1943:	8
1912:	6	1928:	7	1944:	0
1913:	7	1929:	2	1945:	4
1914:	0	1930:	2	1946:	4
1915:	4	1931:	0	1947:	1
1916:	1	1932:	4	1948:	3
1917:	1	1933:	9	1949:	3
1918:	1	1934:	3	1950:	2
1919:	5	1935:	5	1951:	1
1920:	2	1936:	10	1952:	3
1921:	1	1937:	4	1953:	1
1922:	1	1938:	3	1954:	1
1923:	4	1939:	8	1955:	4
1924:	4	1940:	2	1956:	3
1925:	6	1941:	3	1957-61:	0
1926:	5	1942:	6	1962:	1

3. Your court clerk wants to know how burglary case disposition times
   in one court compare to those in other county courtrooms. A random
   sample of 50 burglary cases disposed of during the past year is drawn.

   The data from the random sample of burglary cases (in days):

70	35	86	81	63	71	58	53	99	85
64	56	17	38	94	78	101	71	63	65
58	49	88	70	51	61	80	67	53	74
73	29	64	48	98	78	67	65	76	59
50	65	98	91	66	64	69	86	63	74

   a. Construct an ungrouped frequency distribution.

   b. Calculate the mean, variance and standard deviation.

   c. Compare the following two cases. In your court, case A was dis-
      posed of in 75 days. In another court (with a mean of 61.5 days and
      a standard deviation of 12.5), case B was disposed of in 80 days.

KEY TERMS

frequency distribution

array

measures of central tendency

upper and lower limit

percentiles

variance

standard deviation

normal distribution

parameter

skewness

asymptotic

Z scores

3

GRAPHIC PRESENTATION OF DATA

Graphing is an extremely important element of statistical analysis. It gives greater visibility to the salient features of a distribution and readily suggests the meaning of the data. It also permits rapid and simple interpretation of the data. Graphs can convey an enormous amount of information in a brief format with a great degree of clarity. Graphs can be planned and plotted only after the frequency distribution has been constructed. There are a number of different types of graphs available and most statistical packages for both mainframe and personal computers provide graphics packages.

PIE CHART

Our first example is a pie chart. It is used to demonstrate the percentage of crime types featured in an offender based tracking system (OBTS). Basically, the pie chart uses the 360 degrees of a circle to represent the percentages present in the data. It allows the reader to visually compare the size of the various segments of the data. In Figure 3.1 we can see that the OBTS system collected data on larceny, assault, and burglary cases and that these types of crime were the most frequent in this particular court.

BAR GRAPHS

Bar graphs are usually employed to present data at the nominal and ordinal level of measurement. In our example, seven sets of vertical bars represent the percentage of persons charged as persistent felony offenders (PFOs or career criminals in Kentucky). There are two sets of bars to distinguish between persons charged as PFO I (at least two previous adult convictions) or PFO II (at least one previous adult conviction) for each of seven types of crime (Note: TBUT is larceny-theft). Here we can see that both types of PFOs were comparable in terms of the most serious charge

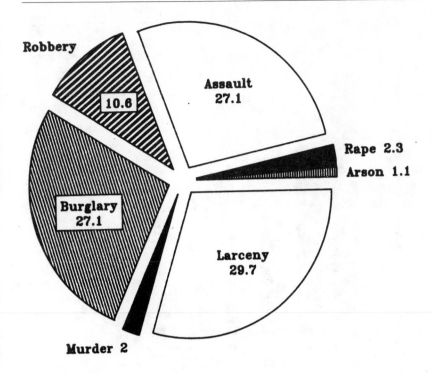

Figure 3.1. OBTS Crimes

of their present offense. These career criminals tended to commit burglary, robbery, and other property offenses.

Bar graphs are also called histograms. In histograms the vertical bars are connected to each other. The height of the columns are proportional to the frequencies in each category and the widths are proportional to the size of the class intervals of the variable. If you use graph paper and draw the bar graph by hand, the following procedure should be followed:

(1) Draw vertical (the *x*-axis or ordinate) and horizontal (the *y*-axis or the abscissa) axes.

(2) On the vertical axis, mark off equal segments which represent the frequencies in the distribution.

(3) Allow for a vacant interval at either end of the horizontal axis. This step improves the appearance of the graph and promotes its readability. The lower limits of the intervals are used to mark the ends of the horizontal scale.

(4) To avoid misrepresentation of the data, the length of the *x* and *y* axes should be roughly equal. The length of the *y*-axis should be approximately ⅔ to ¾

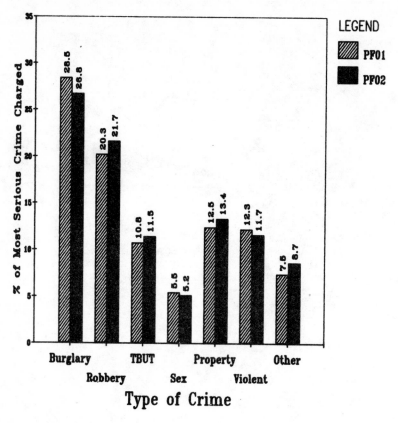

Figure 3.2. Most Serious Charge: Kentucky Persistent Felony Offenders

the length of the x-axis. This rule prevents manipulation of the data to make a weak relationship appear to be a strong one and vice versa.

These steps are excellent guidelines for the construction of all types of graphs and apply to computer generated graphs as well.

FREQUENCY POLYGON

A frequency polygon can be obtained by connecting the midpoints of the bars in a histogram with straight lines (although it is not necessary to construct the histogram first). Frequency polygons portray the shape of the distribution of scores.

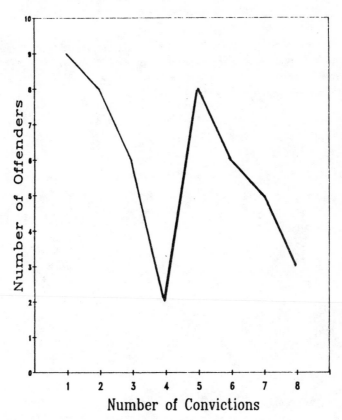

Figure 3.3. Prior Convictions of Repeat Offenders

In Figure 3.3, we have plotted the values for the distribution of prior convictions of repeat offenders presented in Chapter 2. Here, we see an asymmetrical distribution—the two ends of the frequency distribution do not taper off equally. In addition, this distribution tapers off slightly more to the right. The right hand tail of the distribution follows the higher values on the scale. Approximately nine offenders had two prior convictions. In a positively skewed distribution, the mean is always pulled toward the right hand side and the median is located to the left of the mean. Similarly, when the tail of the distribution is pulled to the left of the x-axis, toward the lower values on the scale, it is negatively skewed. In such a distribution, the median tends to lie between the mean and the mode.

SUMMARY

The aim of all graphs is to portray the distribution of data. Graphs can provide a quick look at the data and provide information "at a glance." In this chapter, we briefly presented the three major types of graphs: the pie chart, the bar graph and the frequency polygon.

EXERCISES

1. Using data from Chapter 2, Exercise 1, construct a bar graph.
2. Using data from Chapter 2, Exercise 2, construct a frequency polygon. First, it will be necessary to group the number of executions into five-year intervals.

KEY TERMS

pie chart

bar graph (histogram)

abscissa

ordinate

frequency polygon

REFERENCES

HUFF, D. (1954) *How to lie with statistics.* New York: W. W. Norton.

VITO, G. F., and J. B. ELLIS (1985) *An offender based tracking system study of three judicial districts in the commonwealth of Kentucky.* Louisville: University of Louisville, Kentucky Criminal Justice Statistical Analysis Center.

WILSON, D. G. (1985) *Persistent felony offenders in Kentucky: A profile of the institutional population.* Louisville: University of Louisville, Kentucky Criminal Justice Statistical Analysis Center.

4

PROBABILITY AND SAMPLING

PROBABILITY THEORY

Probabilities originate in uncertainty and provide a basis for coping with it. We deal with them everyday, i.e., What is the chance of rain today? or, to use a criminal justice example, in 1985 the Department of Justice reported that the lifetime risk of being a homicide victim was[1] 1 out of: 179 white males, 30 black males, 495 white females, 132 black females. Probability is the proportion of successes in a large number of trials. Probability of an event:

$$P(s) = \frac{\text{Total Number of Successes}}{\text{Total Number of Outcomes}}$$

(Note: "Success" is not a value judgment, it is what you define it to be.) For example; given one coin, what is the probability of obtaining a head?

$$P = \frac{1}{2} \quad \begin{array}{l} \text{success (H)} \\ \text{number of outcomes (H or T).} \end{array}$$

Probability serves as a basis for inferential statistics (hypothesis testing) and provides a way for coping with uncertainty. Although you may never again have to calculate probabilities, it is important to understand that every statistical table you use to test hypotheses is based upon this concept. A brief look at some basic properties of probabilities will help you to understand how statistical inference operates.

BASIC PROPERTIES OF PROBABILITY

We can obtain no fewer than zero successes and no more than N successes in N trials. For any event A, the probability of A occurring must be greater than or equal to 0 and less than or equal to 1.

The Addition Rule

The probability of any two (or more) outcomes that are mutually exclusive is equal to the sum of their separate probabilities. Mutually exclusive means that the two outcomes cannot possibly occur simultaneously.

$$P(A \text{ or } B) = P(A) + P(B)$$

For example, what is the probability of tossing either a head or a tail in a single flip of one coin?

$$P(A \text{ or } B) = 1/2 + 1/2 = 1$$

What is the probability of rolling a two or four in a single roll of a die?

$$P = 1/6 + 1/6 = 2/6 = 1/3$$

The Multiplication Rule

The probability of the specific outcomes of two or more independent events is equal to the product of their separate probabilities. If the probability of A occurring remains the same regardless of whether or not B has occurred (and if the same holds true for B), the two events are statistically independent of each other. An example would be flipping 3 coins simultaneously. What is the chance of getting a head on all 3 coins?

$$P(A \times B \times C) = P(A)P(B)P(C)$$
$$1/2 \times 1/2 \times 1/2 = 1/8 \text{ or } 12.5\%$$

Note that the multiplication rule can be extended beyond two events.

For events which are not independent; such as the probability of drawing four successive aces from a deck without replacement:

$$P (4 \text{ aces}) = \frac{4}{52} \times \frac{3}{51} \times \frac{2}{50} \times \frac{1}{49} = \frac{1}{270,725}$$

This is an example of conditional probability where the dependent outcome is $P(A \text{ and } B) - P(A)P(B \setminus A)$. Most of the time, we encounter problems that call for us to use both laws together. For example, what is the probability of rolling a seven when shooting dice?

Die 1	Die 2	Die 1	Die 2	Die 1	Die 2
	1		1		1
	2		2	5————2	
	?		3		3
	4	3————4			4
	5		5		5
1————6			6		6
A		B		C	

Die 1	Die 2	Die 1	Die 2	Die 1	Die 2
	1		1	6————1	
	2		2		2
	3	4————3			3
	4		4		4
2————5			5		5
	6		6		6
D		E		F	

The probability of rolling one type of seven (A through F) calls for the use of the Multiplication Rule.

$$P(A) = 1/6 \times 1/6 = 1/36$$
1/6: Probability of rolling a one
1/6: Probability of rolling a six
1/36: Probability of rolling one and six

Then using the Addition Rule:

$$P(A \text{ to } F) = P(A) + P(B) + P(C) + P(D) + P(E) + P(F)$$
$$1/36 + 1/36 + 1/36 + 1/36 + 1/36 + 1/36 = 6/36 = 1/6$$

What is the q (probability of rolling anything but a seven)?

$$P - q = 1.0$$
$$q = 1.0 - P$$
$$q = 1.0 - 1/6$$
$$q = 5/6$$

The Law of Large Numbers is another important aspect of probability. It states that if a situation is repeated again and again, the proportion of successful outcomes will tend to approach the constant probability that any one of the outcomes will be a success. In a string of coin flips, the probability that one of the outcomes will be a success is 1/2. This provides an example of the gambler's fallacy—people believe that the outcome of the previous flip will affect the following one. If the coin is "true," heads and tails are equiprobable. That is, the coin has no memory of the previous outcomes.

CONDITIONAL PROBABILITY

The probability of drawing four successive aces without replacement is an example of conditional probability. The events (drawing aces) are not independent of each other.

$$P(\text{A and B}) = P(\text{A})P(\text{B} \setminus \text{A})$$

where $P(\text{B} \setminus \text{A})$ is the probability of B subject to the conditions that A has occurred. So the probability of drawing two aces in succession is:

$$P(\text{A and B}) = P(\text{A})P(\text{B} \setminus \text{A})$$

$$\frac{4}{52} \times \frac{3}{51} = \frac{12}{2652} = 0.5\%$$

Outcomes which are not mutually exclusive change the rules. Note that the Addition Rule holds true only if the events cannot occur together in a single trial. But, in several instances, an event can be classified in more than one way; an ace can also be a spade. These events are not mutually exclusive, they represent different characteristics of the same event. In this case, the Addition Rule would not apply.

$$P(\text{A or B}) = P(\text{A}) + P(\text{B})$$

$$\frac{4}{52} + \frac{13}{52} = \frac{17}{52} = 32.7\%$$

This probability is too high because we are counting the ace of spades twice. To correct this error, it is necessary to subtract the joint probability (or duplicate occurrence).

$$P(\text{A or B}) = P(\text{A}) + P(\text{B}) - P(\text{A})P(\text{B})$$

$$\frac{4}{52} + \frac{13}{52} - \frac{1}{52} = \frac{16}{52} = 30.8\%$$

Rule: The probability that one of two alternative events, not mutually exclusive, will occur is the sum of the individual probabilities, minus their joint probability.

PERMUTATIONS

Often, you are interested not only in the identity of the elements in the combination, but also in the order of their arrangement. How many ways can eight football teams in a conference be ranked at the end of the season.

$$8 \quad 7 \quad 6 \quad 5 \quad 4 \quad 3 \quad 2 \quad 1$$

The first slot can be filled by any of the teams, the second by 7 teams, etc. Through the use of the multiplication theorem: If an event can occur in N ways, and thereafter in N_2 ways, and so on, these events can occur in that order in $N_1 \times N_2 \ldots Nn$ ways. So

$$8 \times 7 \times 6 \times 5 \times 4 \times 3 \times 2 \times 1 = 40{,}320$$

Complete Permutation consists of permutating all objects in a set, all at a time or N objects, N at a time. The resulting number of permutations is called the factorial of the number as symbolized: $P = N!$ Partial Permutation consists of N objects taken r at a time, in other words, r equals some number less than N. Given 9 criminals, how many different permutations can fill the first four cells in the local jail?

$$\frac{9 \times 8 \times 7 \times 6 \times 5 \times 4 \times 3 \times 2 \times 1}{5 \times 4 \times 3 \times 2 \times 1} = 3{,}024$$

THE BINOMIAL DISTRIBUTION

Suppose you have an event with two possible outcomes that are mutually exclusive (either you have it or you don't, you are or you aren't). Such an event is called a binomial. Where,

$$p = \text{probability of success}$$

and

$$q = 1 - p, \text{ probability of failure}$$

One way to figure the results (and avoid tedium) is to use the Binomial Coefficient formula:

$$(p + q)^n$$

where p = one outcome (heads)
         q = the other outcome (tails)
         n = number of events

So, for two coins:

$$(p + q)^2 \quad = \quad p^2 \quad + \quad 2pq \quad + \quad q^2$$

| 1 outcome of | 2 outcomes of | 1 outcome of |
| 2 heads | 1 head, 1 tail | 2 tails |

For three coins: $(p + q)^3 =$

$$p^3 \quad + \quad 3p^2q \quad + \quad 3pq^2 \quad + \quad q^3$$

| 1 of 3 heads | 3 of 2 heads | 3 of 2 tails | 1 of 3 tails |
| | 1 tail | 1 head | |

The binomial distribution is concerned with the probability of sequences of outcomes for dichotomous (two mutually exclusive parts—success or failure) events. The important assumption of the binomial distribution is that each outcome is independent of other outcomes. P (probability of success) is assumed to remain unchanged. Therefore, its application may be somewhat limited. The binomial distribution approaches normality as N increases.

BASICS OF SAMPLING

Generally, the criminal justice researcher conducts his or her analysis on the basis of limited information. Due to the constraints of time and money, it is generally impossible to collect data from an entire universe, so a sample is constructed. Thus, sampling involves the selection of a portion of the universe and an attempt to draw a conclusion about the universe based on analysis of the sample. (Note: The universe is also called the population). For example, it would be virtually impossible to study all the prisoners housed in our prisons; however, we could draw a sample of prisoners and study that sample. Of course, the most common example of sampling involves polling at election time, in which a relatively small number of registered voters is asked about their voting preferences. Fortunately, pollsters have the luxury of finding out if their samples were accurate—election day!

No matter how the sample is selected, there are two possible sources of error (1) probability or chance error, and (2) systematic bias: selecting the sample from only one point of the universe. There are two basic types of samples; probability, in which every member of the population is given an equal chance of being selected, and nonprobability, in which not all members of the population are given an equal chance.

SAMPLING METHODS: A FEW BRIEF EXAMPLES

Simple Random

Assign to each population member a unique number. This is called constructing a sampling list. Next, select sample members through the use of a table of random numbers, or pull them out of a hat. This procedure provides an equal opportunity of selection to each unit in the population. It is also the basis of experimental research—the construction of experimental and control groups to evaluate the effectiveness of a treatment.

Stratified Random

Divide the population into strata (e.g., blacks, whites, Chicanos in prison) and select a random sample within each strata proportionate to the size of the strata in the population. In other words, if 50% of the prison population is black, 45% white and 5% Chicano, you would divide your sampling list into the appropriate strata and randomly select blacks, whites, and Chicanos proportionate to their percentage in the population.

Due to cost, human subject research restrictions, and the state of the criminal justice system information and data, random samples are becoming ever more difficult to obtain. As a result, many researchers are forced to develop samples that are not truly random. Several examples of nonrandom samples are as follows.

Availability Sampling

Selecting a sample from readily available subjects. Often the researcher is faced with the distasteful decision to either go with what is available or abandon the study. For example, delinquency studies of readily available (incarcerated) delinquents. Many researchers would not scrap a study because of their inability to acquire or construct a random sample. Availability samples may be acceptable, providing the researcher clearly states his or her reasons for using this technique.

Matching

In some cases a researcher may not be able to randomly assign subjects to groups. This is often the case in criminal justice. For example, judges usually decide whether or not an offender should be placed in a treatment program. In order to develop a comparison group, matching is often used. This technique involves selected cases for a control group based on some characteristics, such as gender, race, risk, and so forth.

Judgment Samples

This procedure involves taking the group which seems to be representative of all members and studying that group. For example, it would be virtually impossible to draw a random sample of the Hell's Angels; however, you might be able to study one chapter of the group. However, the assumption is unlikely to be true that the group you chose to study is fairly similar to other chapters.

Accidental Sample

Take whomever comes along. This is the "man on the street" approach often used by newspeople.

The types of samples listed above are very basic and elementary; however, for our purposes they should be sufficient.[2]

SAMPLING DISTRIBUTIONS

Although sampling techniques are more commonly associated with research methods than statistical analysis, as you shall see, the general logic is important in helping to understand sampling distributions. The usefulness of a sample is directly related to the ability of the sample to provide information and a description of the population from which it is drawn. The problem is that no two samples are alike, and all are in error, so with how much confidence can the researcher speak about the value of the universe? This problem is dealt with through the use of a set of prescribed procedures known as statistical inference. Basically, statistical inference means that the researcher wishes to infer something about a population by examining a sample of elements taken from it. To insure accuracy the following procedures are suggested:

(1) Make sure that each element in the parent population is identified or known. Of course, this is one of the requirements of random sampling, the construction of a sampling list. When you are unable to reach or select certain members of a population, the resulting sample is considered biased. It will be unrepresentative of the population from which it is drawn.

(2) Draw a random sample whenever possible.

(3) Draw a sample of sufficient size to permit you to make accurate generalizations about the larger population. (A mathematical argument. As we shall see, due to the law of large numbers, increasing sample size causes the sampling distribution of the mean to approach a normal distribution. Thus, several statistical tests recommend that $N > 30$ be used. If $N < 30$, other tests would be more appropriate.)

In sum, statistical inference is the process of saying something about a large population of elements as a consequence of examining a sample of these elements. Always remember that errors in sampling will accompany almost every technique (even random sampling), but these errors (when taken on the whole) behave systematically. Even when you are not intimately familiar with the population, you can be assured that the sample statistic will be somewhat representative of the population parameter.

The Sampling Distribution of a Statistic refers to the theoretical probability distribution of that statistic. The sampling distribution of a statistic involves a mathematical concept. The first step is to draw all possible samples of a given size (*N*) that can be drawn from the population in question. The sampling distribution of the statistic is the distribution of the value of the statistic within each sample. For example, the number of prior arrests for convicted burglars. Given the number of prior arrests as 6, 9, 11, 14, draw a random sample of two without replacement.

Sample Number	Sample	Mean
1	6, 9	7.5
2	6, 11	8.5
3	6, 14	10.0
4	9, 11	10.0
5	9, 14	11.5
6	9, 6	7.5
7	11, 6	8.5
8	11, 9	10.0
9	11, 14	12.5
10	14, 6	10.0
11	14, 9	11.5
12	14, 11	12.5

According to the "magic" theorem for the sampling distribution of the mean, if repeated random samples of size *n* are drawn from a normal population, with mean (μ) and variance (σ^2), the sampling distribution of sample means will be normal, with mean (μ) and variance = σ^2/N. Here, we can determine the actual population mean.

$$6 + 9 + 11 + 14 = 40/4 = 10.$$

So, the population mean is 10, the population variance is 8.5 and the population standard deviation is 2.9. If we plot the distribution of sample means, the result will be a normal curve. Returning to our example:

$\overline{X}$	f
12.5	2
11.5	2
10.0	4
8.5	2
7.5	2
	$N = 12$

of samples

The larger the sample size selected, the smaller the standard deviation in the sampling distribution of the mean. The standard deviation of the sampling distribution of the mean is referred to as the Standard Error of the Mean. If the sample size were increased, the size of the standard error of the mean would decrease. This is one reason why researchers like to use large samples. They reduce the size of the standard error, or the error involved when estimating a parameter by using a sample statistic.

THE CENTRAL LIMIT THEOREM

We have previously stated that, if the sample size is large, the sampling distribution of the mean approximates the normal distribution. Thus, the Central Limit Theorem: If repeated random samples of size N are drawn from any population having a mean (μ), and a variance, (σ^2) then as N increases, the sampling distribution of sample means approaches normality. This theorem applies when N is sufficiently large (at least over 30), and provided that the resulting sampling distribution will be approximately normal. Since this sampling distribution will be used in significance testing, the assumption about the normality of the population can be relaxed.

ESTABLISHING CONFIDENCE LIMITS

If you remember the size of the areas under the normal curve (Z scores), the sampling distribution of the mean is approximately normal around the population mean (μ); therefore, two out of every three sample means (68.26%) will lie within one standard error of the true mean. In other words, the sample mean has 2 chances in 3 of falling within one standard error of the population mean. Similarly, 95 out of 100 sample means lie within 1.96 standard errors of the true population mean. Or, if we attach 1.96 standard errors to either side of the sample mean, we have a 95% probability of enclosing the population mean. This method does not disclose the exact location of the population mean, it merely gives some indication that the population mean will be found within the specified interval derived from the observed sample. We are usually interested in knowing the proximity of the parameter to the statistic which we have computed. Although the population parameter is unknown, we can make a good guess from the knowledge of the sample statistic. The standard error of the mean is used to establish a reasonable distance within which the population parameter will lie (given a certain level of probability). Given the mean and the standard deviation of a distribution of scores, we are able to specify how far above or below the mean we must go, in standard deviation units, in order to include a certain proportion of cases. Knowledge of the standard error of the mean also permits us to specify how far above or below the sample mean we must go, in terms of standard errors, in order to include a certain proportion of sample means.

A confidence interval is an interval established around the sample mean, which includes a given proportion of sample means and which includes the population mean at a certain level of probability. If we are willing to have the population parameter excluded from the confidence interval 10% of the time, we should establish a 90% confidence limit. The same logic applies to the 95% confidence limit. Since a confidence interval extends an equal distance on either side of the sample mean, we are interested in obtaining a Z value which will cut off a given distance from the mean, leaving the desired percent of the area (5%) in the tails of the distribution. For example, the 95% confidence interval splits the remaining 5% into two equal parts, leaving 2.5% of the curve at each end of the distribution. Using the Table A "Areas Under the Normal Curve," we are looking for a Z value which includes the proportion .4750. This value is ± 1.96. Thus, the 95% confidence interval: $\overline{X} \pm (1.96)(S_{\overline{x}})$ (where: $S_{\overline{x}} = \dfrac{s'}{\sqrt{N}}$). For the 99% confidence interval, the Z score would be ± 2.58. The 95% and 99% confidence intervals are used by researchers more than all others.

Basically, the use of the confidence intervals is rather simple. The first decision to be made is whether or not you are willing to take the risk of making the error of stating that the parameter is somewhere in the interval when in fact it is not. There are two types of sample means (1) those that do not fall within the critical region, (2) those that do fall within the critical region. Given the two means ($\overline{X}_1$ and $\overline{X}_2$), if we place 1.96 standard units on either side of both means (the 95% confidence interval), we can see that $\overline{X}_2$ would enclose the population mean (μ), but $\overline{X}_1$ would not. It is important to remember that with the confidence interval we are really referring to the probability of obtaining a particular value; 95% of the time we will obtain intervals (or yield sample means) close enough to the parameter that the confidence intervals obtained will actually include the population mean. Why the 95% and 99% confidence intervals? First of all, there is absolutely nothing sacred about them. They are a product of convention. However, the wider the interval, the less reliable it is. For example, saying that

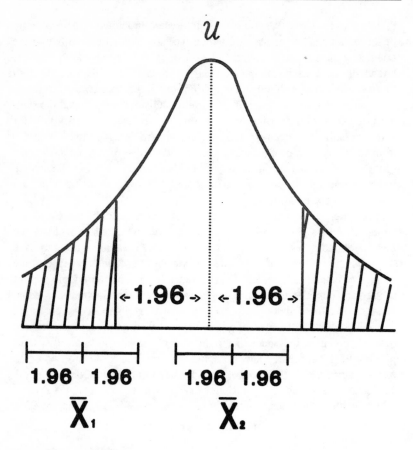

Figure 4.1. Normal Distribution

the mean salary for police officers in Chicago lies between $5,000 and $40,000 is not very informative. On the other hand, if the interval is too narrow, the probability of error increases. Therefore, the 95% and 99% levels are attempts to obtain a balance and state with some "confidence" that the population mean is contained within the interval.

SUMMARY

This chapter has covered the principles of probability, the basics of sampling and sampling distributions, the central limit theorem and confidence limits. It is important to understand that this material serves as a foundation for statistical testing and, in particular, hypothesis testing.

It is usually impossible to study an entire population. As a result, we want our sample to be representative of the population. In other words, we want to be relatively confident of our sample statistic. What are the chances? Of course, that involves probability. What we are generally trying to do is infer something about a population based on a sample. This is statistical inference. We have also learned that numbers tend to behave in a certain way, particularly when the N is sufficiently large. That is the Central Limit Theorem. In the next chapter, we will see how all this fits into hypothesis testing.

NOTES

[1] From *Report to the Nation on Crime and Justice, 2nd.* (1988) U.S. Department of Justice, Bureau of Justice Statistics, pg. 28.

[2] For a more detailed examination of sampling see Babbie, E. R. *Survey Research Methods,* (Belmont, CA: Wadsworth) 1973; Vito, G. F., Latessa, E. J. and Wilson, D. *Introduction to Criminal Research Methods,* (Springfield, IL: Charles C Thomas), 1988.

EXERCISES

1. What is the probability of rolling an eight when shooting dice?
2. What are the odds of rolling anything but an eight?
3. What is the probability of drawing three kings in succession?
4. You have ten police officers and four walkie-talkies. How many different permutations are there for the walkie talkies?
5. What is the binomial distribution used for?
6. What are the two basic types of samples?
7. What is random sampling and how does it differ from availability sampling? Judgment sampling?
8. What are the prescribed procedures for statistical inference?
9. What is the sampling distribution of a statistic?
10. What is the standard error of the mean?
11. What is the Central Limit Theorem? When does it apply?
12. What is a confidence limit and why do we establish them?
13. What are the conventional confidence limits? Why don't we make them narrower? Broader?

KEY TERMS

addition rule

multiplication rule

conditional probability

law of large numbers

permutations

binomial distribution

probability error

systematic bias

random sample

nonrandom sample

central limit theorem

confidence limits

5

HYPOTHESIS TESTING

This chapter will examine the fundamentals of hypothesis testing as it relates to statistical testing. As we shall see, hypothesis testing is a very important part of the research process. Statistical testing consists of two types; estimation and hypothesis testing.

Estimation. We have demonstrated this concept in our study of confidence limits. We began with a sample mean and then, within a specified degree of confidence, made an estimate of an interval which would contain the population mean. In this manner, an interval estimate begins with sample data and ends with a range of values which probably includes the population mean. An example of this is political polling in which an estimation is made concerning the outcome of an election. Pollsters have the luxury of finding out whether or not their estimates are accurate—election day!

Hypothesis Testing. Hypothesis testing begins with a hypothesis about the parameter and then uses the sample data to test the accuracy of the hypothesis. Thus, hypothesis testing begins with an assumption about a population value and ends with a decision to reject or accept the hypothesis on the basis of the sample data. There are several different types of hypotheses.

RESEARCH HYPOTHESES

Research hypotheses are derived from theories held by the researcher or derived from other sources. They generally state a specified relation between two or more variables, or they are tentatively held suppositions about what is, how things change, or how events are interrelated. For example, you might theorize that there is a relationship between children from broken families and delinquency. A research hypothesis could easily be developed and tested that examined this premise.

A statistical hypothesis is a statement, assertion, or claim about the nature of a population. So the research hypothesis generally must be stated in statistical form in order to be tested. One form of statistical hypothesis is the Null Hypothesis—the hypothesis of no difference (designated as H_0).

The H_0 is formulated with the full expectation that it will be rejected or "nullified." Usually, the research hypothesis is supported when it is nullified and is unsupported when we fail to nullify it. Therefore, the null hypothesis is tested against the research (or alternative) hypothesis (H_1).

> H_0: There is no difference in the number of traffic fatalities before and after the passage of a new mandatory seat belt law.
>
> H_1: The number of traffic fatalities decreases following the passage of a new mandatory seat belt law.

A test of a statistical hypothesis is a rule or procedure that leads to a decision to accept or to reject the hypothesis when the experimental sample values are obtained. These rules are called Decision Rules and they help us to decide how to judge the observations contained in the data. Decision rules involve specifying the sampling distribution of a statistic, the level of significance, and the region of rejection in the sampling distribution.

If you remember our examples from the standard error of the mean, a sampling distribution of a statistic is the distribution of all possible values that any statistic may assume, based upon random sampling of a specified size from a specified universe. In turn, this distribution specifies probabilities associated with the occurrence of any statistical value. Thus, decision rules involve the specification or identification of a sampling distribution which will help in the support or rejection of statistical hypotheses.

TESTING THE NULL (H_0) HYPOTHESIS

One important principle of this procedure is that we can never prove the null hypothesis true. This is due to the fact that even if we found or obtained a sample value precisely equal to our hypothesized value, we could still not be positive that H_0 was true. Why? This result could be due to sampling error. By the same token, we can never be absolutely sure that H_0 is false, but the statistical evidence may be more convincing when the null hypothesis can be rejected within a certain range of probability. The level of significance refers to the probability that we are wrong in rejecting H_0. If we hypothesize that there is no difference between two sample means at the .05 level of significance and there is a difference at this level, we are saying that 5 times out of 100 we are wrong in rejecting H_0. When testing hypotheses, we have two possibilities regarding H_0. H_0 is true, or H_0 is false. If the H_0 is true and we reject it, we have committed a Type I error. The probability of committing this error is denoted by the Greek letter α (alpha) and is referred to as the level of significance. Accept H_0; correct decision probability = $1 - \alpha$. If the H_0 is true and we reject H_0 we have made an incorrect decision probability = α. If the H_0 is false, and we accept it, we have committed a Type II error. Its probability is denoted by the Greek letter β (beta).

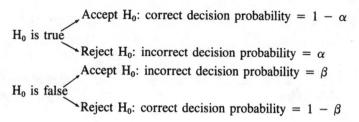

$$\text{Accept } H_0: \text{ correct decision probability} = 1 - \alpha$$
$$H_0 \text{ is true}$$
$$\text{Reject } H_0: \text{ incorrect decision probability} = \alpha$$
$$\text{Accept } H_0: \text{ incorrect decision probability} = \beta$$
$$H_0 \text{ is false}$$
$$\text{Reject } H_0: \text{ correct decision probability} = 1 - \beta$$

Note that the researcher, prior to his or her analysis, determines the level of significance in the study. So why not cheat? If you set the level of significance too low, .10, .20, .50, you increase the probability of Type I error (α). If you set it too high, .001 or .0001 to increase accuracy, you also increase probability of Type II error (β). So, the necessity of compromise has lead to the "sacred cow" of the .05 level of significance. For example, a jury trial requires proof beyond reasonable doubt to prove guilt. H_1: The defendant is guilty; or H_0: The defendant is not guilty. The prosecution sets out to destroy the null hypothesis. Also, if the accused goes free, it does not mean that the defendant is innocent. This example illustrates the aura of probability surrounding H_0.

	Innocent	Guilty
Acquitted	True	Type I error
Convicted	Type II	True

REGION OF REJECTION

The region of rejection consists of those sample values (located in one or both tails of the distribution) whose combined probability under the null hypothesis is equal to α. As Figure 5.1-1 illustrates, the regions of rejection are found in the tails of the distribution. This figure also represents a two-tailed test. In Figure 5.1-2, we can see that to locate the region of rejection in a two-tailed test, we divide α (.05) in half. Thus, with $\alpha = .05$, we find the Z value that marks off the extreme .025 area in each tail. Recall that under the normal curve, the Z value associated with .05 level is 1.96. Finally, Figure 5.1-3 demonstrates a one-tailed test involving one end of the normal curve. A Z score of 1.64 marks off .4500% of the scores, leaving .05 in the tail. Thus, 1.64 is a critical value of Z for a one-tailed test at the .05 level. The use of a one-tailed versus a two-tailed test is determined by the ability to make a prediction regarding the direction of our

Figure 1—Normal Distributions

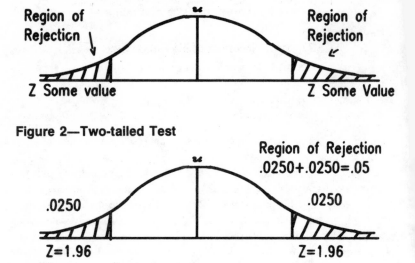

Figure 2—Two-tailed Test

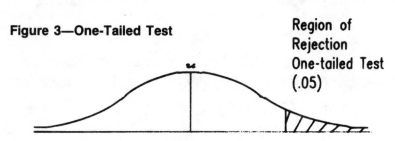

Figure 3—One-Tailed Test

Figure 5.1. Normal Distribution Showing Critical Regions

hypothesis. It is often possible to predict directions on the basis of either a theory or previous studies, i.e., persons with a prior record are more likely to commit another crime. However, when a researcher has started out with insufficient information to formulate a more precise directional hypothesis, then a two-tailed test is appropriate. Unless the research has strong support for predicting direction it is usually better to develop a two-tailed hypothesis.

In sum, the decision to reject or accept is based upon the location of the test statistic in its sampling distribution. If it is located in the region of rejection, as determined by alpha (α), the H_0 can be rejected. Note that statistical significance can tell us only that certain sample differences would not occur very frequently by chance if there were no differences whatsoever in the population. It tells us nothing directly about the magnitude of these differences and it does not measure the degree of relationship.

STEPS OF HYPOTHESIS TESTING

(1) State your research hypothesis.

(2) State the null hypothesis.

(3) Choose an appropriate statistical test, one for which all required assumptions can be met.

(4) Specify a significance level (α) and a sample size (N).

    a. Remember, probability of Type I error = α and probability of Type II error = β.

    b. Since α and N are specified in advance, β is determined. The inverse relationship between the two probabilities is such that decrease in α will increase β for a given N. To reduce the probability of both types of errors, it is necessary to increase N.

    c. This concept is related to the Power of a Test—the probability of rejecting H_0 when it is false or $1 - \beta$. The power of a test increases as N increases.

(5) Find or assume the sampling distribution of the statistical test under the H_0. This is done in order to make probability statements about certain values associated with the statistic.

(6) On the basis of 1, 3 and 4, define the region of rejection.

(7) Compute the value of the statistical test, using the data obtained from the sample.

(8) Make a decision regarding the null hypothesis and interpret the findings.

NONPARAMETRIC VERSUS PARAMETRIC STATISTICS

The choice of a particular statistical test generally depends on whether or not certain assumptions are met. For example, as you learned earlier, level of measurement is one of the critical factors in deciding what statistical test to use. Other factors also play a part in deciding about a particular test. While there are many statistical tests to choose from, they fall into one of two basic types.

Parametric Tests

The parametric tests are the most powerful tests available. You should use them whenever possible. However, parametric tests specify certain conditions about the parameters from which the research sample was drawn.

(1) Observations must be independent. The selection of any one case from th population for the sample must not bias the chances of any other case fc selection.

(2) Observations must be drawn from normally distributed populations.

(3) Populations should have equal variances (called homogeneity of variance).

(4) The data should be at the interval or ratio level of measurement.

(5) Additive effects.

Before any confidence can be placed in the probability statement obtained by the use of a parametric test these conditions should be met. These are the assumptions behind the use of parametric statistical tests. Since these conditions are not ordinarily tested, they are assumed to hold. However, the meaningfulness of the results of a parametric test depends upon the validity of these assumptions.

We can avoid having to meet these assumptions without losing power by choosing a different test and drawing a larger N. In this manner, we can avoid having to make assumptions and still retain the power to reject H_0. Basically, we are talking about the power of a statistic. Power = $1 - \beta$ (Beta). In other words, the greater the power, the less the probability of accepting a false null hypothesis.

Nonparametric Tests

A nonparametric statistical test is a test whose model does not specify conditions about the parameters of the population from which the sample was drawn. The disadvantage is that if the assumptions are met, then nonparametric tests tend to waste data. So what do you do in practice? Meet as many of the assumptions as you can but, nonparametric statistics allow you to relax these assumptions. This is the major advantage of nonparametric statistics. Or, as Siegel (1956) argues, by increasing the size of your sample, you can increase the power of nonparametric statistics to equal that of parametric tests.

A nonparametric statistical test is one whose model does not specify the conditions about the parameters of the population from which the sample was drawn. There are four major advantages of nonparametric tests:

(1) Probability statements obtained from most nonparametric tests are exact probabilities, regardless of the shape of the population distribution from which the random sample was drawn.

(2) Small samples can be used ($N = 6$ or less). This is impossible with parametric statistics.

(3) No assumption is made about homogeneity of variance.

(4) They can be used at any level of measurement.

Nonparametric tests provide an alternative when assumptions cannot be met, so you don't have to let assumptions stand in your way. If your hypothesis is important and requires a violation, do it, provided that you are aware that the assumptions are being violated and you know the effects of the violation. The following simple rules will help you when testing hypotheses

(1) Always remember to use the classic probability levels (.05 or .01), unless you have a strong reason not to.
(2) Use as large a sample as possible.
(3) Choose the population before you select the sample.
(4) Use the simplest statistic which answers the hypothesis (this means of course that you must know precisely what the hypothesis states).
(5) Choose a flip-flop hypothesis whenever possible, one that is important regardless of whether the findings are significant or not.

Table 5.1 illustrates some of the more common parametric and nonparametric tests and the corresponding levels of measurement.

TABLE 5.1. Appropriate Statistical Tests: Some Brief Examples

Scale	*Examples of Appropriate Statistics*	
Nominal and Ordinal	Mode Frequencies Median Percentile Spearman's Rho Chi-Square	NONPARAMETRIC STATISTICAL TESTS
Interval and Ratio	Mean Standard Deviation Pearson's *r* *t* TEST ANOVA Regression	NONPARAMETRIC* AND PARAMETRIC TESTS

*Remember, it is appropriate to use nonparametric tests with interval and ratio level data, but the results usually waste information.

SUMMARY

This chapter has examined the basics of hypothesis testing and the assumptions surrounding the use of parametric and nonparametric statistics. Hypothesis testing is a critical component of scientific research.

A hypothesis is an expectation about the nature of things derived from a theory. It is a statement that ought to be observed in the real world if the theory is correct. Hypothesis testing involves determining whether the expectations are, in fact, present in the real world.

Now that you have a basic understanding of some of the concepts and logic involved in statistical testing we can turn our attention to some of the more common statistical tests used in criminal justice research.

EXERCISES

1. What are the steps of hypothesis testing?
2. What are the differences between nonparametric and parametric statistics?
3. How can the power of a nonparametric statistic be increased?
4. Can the null hypothesis be proven true? Explain?
5. Why are nonparametric statistics so useful?

KEY TERMS

estimation

hypothesis

null hypothesis

region of rejection

Type I error

Type II error

REFERENCE

Siegel, S. (1956) *Nonparametric statistics for the behavioral sciences.* New York: McGraw-Hill.

6

THE *t*-DISTRIBUTION AND *t* TEST

Remember that the Central Limit Theorem states that, if sample size N is large, the sample statistic approaches the Z distribution. In other words, when you take a sample from a normally distributed population with a *known* mean (μ) and standard deviation (σ), and then compute a Z score on the basis of each observation, the resulting scores will have a Z distribution—normal distribution with mean = 0 and standard deviation = 1. The problem is that, in most cases, we never know the value of the population standard deviation (σ). Since the Central Limit Theorem involves the use of the standard deviation (σ), it cannot be ignored. One solution is to substitute the sample standard deviation (s') for the population standard deviation (σ).

This is exactly the problem that faced William S. Gossett in 1908. Gossett was hired by a famous English brewery to establish quality control procedures for the brewing of ale. Faced with small samples, Gossett developed the following statistic, making use of the previously mentioned distribution:

$$\text{Student's } t\text{-distribution: } t = \frac{\overline{X} - \mu}{s'/\sqrt{N}}$$

Gossett used the pen name "student" when he published his findings concerning the use of this statistic. This secrecy was necessary, since the brewery legally owned the fruits of Gossett's labor. Hence, the "t" statistic. The t-distribution is a continuous sampling distribution which is similar to the normal distribution in several respects. It is symmetrical, has a mean of zero, but its exact pattern depends on a parameter called Degrees of Freedom.

Degrees of freedom is another important statistical concept that we will encounter again and again. Several simple examples and definitions follow. If we force three values to add to 12, we can write two of the values arbitrarily, but the third will be determined by the requirement that the 3 values = 12.

$$X + Y + Z = 12$$

If we say that $X = 4$, $Y = 5$, then Z *must equal* 3.

$$4 + 5 + 3 = 12$$

Since only X and Y are *free to vary*, we say that in this case, the degrees of freedom equal two.

Or, if we have n independent observations and each observation is free to vary in a possible range, these observations have n degrees of freedom. When certain restrictions are placed upon these observations, the number of degrees of freedom is reduced. With the t-distribution, this quantity is $N - 1$. The degrees of freedom determine the shape of the t-distribution. The t-distribution also differs from the Z-distribution in that the area under its tail regions is larger than in the normal distribution. This is especially true when the sample size n is small.

In Figure 6.1, the t-distribution (for sample size of 6) is flatter and wider than the Z, or unit normal, distribution. Ten percent of the t scores, as compared with 5% of the Z scores, are $> +2$. This is due to the variability introduced when we replaced the sample standard deviation (s') for population standard deviation (σ) in the Central Limit Theorem. As Table B demonstrates, the values of t get close to the corresponding Z values (1.96 at the 95% confidence interval), as their size or degrees of freedom increase. Note that the value of t at the .05 level (infinity) is 1.96. So, with larger numbers of degrees of freedom, the curve for the t-distribution rises at the center, getting close to the unit normal (Z) distribution. Calculation of confidence limits under the t-distribution follows the same form as the Z-distribution where:

$$(s\bar{x}) = \frac{s'}{\sqrt{N - 1}}$$

CI 95 $= X \pm$ (t value) ($s\bar{x}$ = standard error of the mean)

Except that for the t-distribution, with every degree of freedom, the nature and areas under the curve (size of) change. Consider the following example where:

$$N = 20$$
$$s\bar{x} = 3.5$$
$$\overline{X} = 50$$

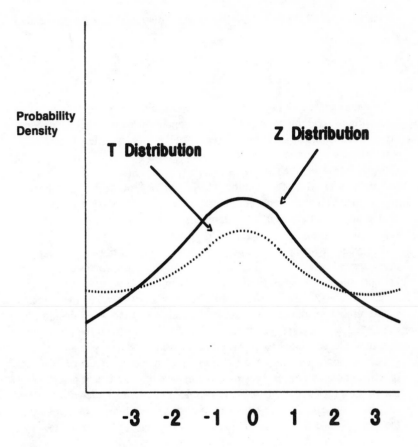

Figure 6.1. T Distribution

The first step is to calculate the degrees of freedom ($N - 1$):

$$20 - 1 = 19.$$

Now, using Table B, we determine the t value that corresponds to the 95% (2.09) and 99% (2.54) confidence levels. Using our formula:

$$CI95 = 50 \pm (2.09)(3.5)$$
$$CI99 = 50 \pm (2.54)(3.5)$$

The interpretation of these confidence intervals is no different than the Z score method. We can be 95% confident that the population mean (μ) lies in the interval 42.69 to 57.32. Use of the t-distribution is recommended for small samples ($N < 30$).

t TEST

Often, our research questions involve examining the difference between two samples of elements. (1) Are delinquent children more likely to come from broken homes? (2) Does one region of the country differ from another with respect to homicide rates? The statistical implication here is that the difference between the two groups is significant. With a test of significance, we are interested in determining whether or not the probability that the observed differences were caused by chance alone. The .05 level limits the probability that the observed differences were caused by chance alone 5 times out of 100.

The type of test chosen will depend upon whether or not the two samples are independent or nonindependent (related). Related samples occur when (1) both samples have been matched according to some trait, i.e., race or gender, are a (2) linked relationship (brother and sister), or (3) repeated measurements of the same sample (before-after or time series design). Independent samples are selected in such a way as to permit the assumption that they are unrelated to one another according to any variable.

Let's suppose that we have two groups of inmates, one over 50 years of age and one under 50. We want to compare the number of prior felony convictions for each group. Note, that t does not assume a negative value, so when you calculate a t test either position your sample means so that the largest mean is first or simply ignore the sign of your t value.

Inmates 50 and older	Inmates 18-49
$N = 33$	$N = 19$
$\overline{X} = 3.2$	$\overline{X} = 4.9$
Sum of Squares $= 87$	Sum of Squares $= 99$

First we must obtain the "pooled variance":

$$s'^2 = \frac{\Sigma x_1^2 + \Sigma x_2^2}{N_1 + N_2 - 2} = \frac{87 + 99}{33 + 19 - 2} = \frac{186}{50} = 3.72$$

This amounts to a "pooling" of the standard errors of each of the means in order that we may more properly evaluate the differences between them. The pooling takes into account the differences in sample sizes and the differences in standard deviations or variance. Next, we calculate the standard error of the difference:

$$s\bar{x}_1 - \bar{x}_2 = \sqrt{\frac{s^2}{N_1} + \frac{s^2}{N^2}} = \sqrt{\frac{3.72}{33} + \frac{3.72}{19}} = 0.56$$

Finally, calculate the t test.

$$t = \frac{\overline{X}_1 - \overline{X}_2}{s\bar{x}_1 - \bar{x}_2} = \frac{4.9 - 3.2}{0.56} = \frac{1.7}{0.56} = 3.04$$

Using Table B, our decision would be to reject the null hypothesis and to conclude that younger inmates have more prior felony convictions than older inmates.

t Test for Related Samples

Suppose a police chief wishes to know if his cadets are learning about police work at the police academy. He tests them at the very beginning of their training, and then again after they have completed the academy.

Individual	Test #1	Test #2	D	D²
A	63	68	5	25
B	41	49	8	64
C	54	53	−1	1
D	71	75	4	16
E	39	49	10	100
F	44	41	−3	9
G	67	75	8	64
H	56	58	2	4
I	61	55	−6	36
$N = 9$	$\Sigma X_1 = 496$	$\Sigma X_2 = 523$	$\Sigma D = 27$	$\Sigma D^2 = 319$

Here, you would subtract the score on test #1 from the score on test #2 because, if the training is effective and a cadet learns about police work, his or her score on the second test (after the training) should be higher than the score on the first test (before the training).

First compute the mean for each group:

$$\overline{X}_1 = \frac{\Sigma X_1}{N} = \frac{496}{9} = 55.11 \qquad \overline{X}_2 = \frac{\Sigma X_2}{N} = \frac{523}{9} = 58.11$$

Now compute the population variance of difference scores:

$$S_D^2 = \frac{N\Sigma D^2 - (\Sigma D)^2}{N(N-1)} = \frac{9(319) - (27)^2}{9(8)} = \frac{2142}{72} = 29.75$$

Next compute the estimation of the Population Standard Error of the Mean Difference Scores:

$$S_D = \sqrt{\frac{S_D{}^2}{N}} = \sqrt{\frac{29.75}{9}} = \sqrt{3.305} = 1.82$$

Finally, calculate the t test:

$$t = \frac{\overline{X}_1 - \overline{X}_2}{S_D} = \frac{55.11 - 58.11}{1.82} = \frac{3}{1.82} = 1.65$$

$$df = 9 - 1 = 8$$

Using Table B, at the .05 level our decision would be to accept the null hypothesis and conclude that the police cadets had not learned about police work at the academy.

Remember, the t test is especially appropriate with small samples (fewer than 30). Typically, a Z test is used with larger samples. However, if the N is greater than 30 you can still calculate a t test and then simply use Table B to determine acceptance or rejection of the H_0. In other words, treat your t value as if it were a Z score. Remember, with a $N > 30$, the t value approximates the normal distribution, so t and Z become increasingly equivalent in function.

In interpreting the t test you should remember that the magnitude of the t is not necessarily indicative of the magnitude of the difference between the means. A statistically significant difference does not necessarily indicate a cause and effect relationship, and the statistical inference drawn should be limited to the population sampled.

DIFFERENCES BETWEEN PROPORTIONS TEST

The difference between two proportions, drawn from the same sample, can be treated as a special case of the difference between two means. The Difference Between Proportions test is similar to the t test in that it can be used with a very small sample. The procedure for testing the null hypothesis is identical, in fundamentals, with that procedure we have studied for testing the difference between two means with the t test.

In his study of the variables related to the decision to grant shock probation, Vito discovered that among 243 cases, 41.7% of the whites (58/139) and 32.6% of the nonwhites (34/104) were released. Research Hypothesis: A higher percentage of whites are granted release on shock probation.

(Racial Discrimination?) (Note that direction is predicted.) Null Hypothesis: There is no difference in the percentage of shock probationers released.

First, we must determine the pooled estimate of the parameter proportion.

$$P = \frac{F_1 + F_2}{N_1 + N_2}$$

F_1 = number of individuals in first group
F_2 = number of individuals in second group

$$\frac{58 + 34}{139 + 104} = \frac{92}{243} \quad P = .379$$

Next, we determine q.

$q = 1 - p.$
$1 - .379 = .621$

Then we determine the standard error of the proportion (S_{D_p}):

$$S_{D_p} = \sqrt{pq \left(\frac{1}{N_1} + \frac{1}{N_2} \right)} = \sqrt{(.379)(.621) \left(\frac{1}{139} + \frac{1}{104} \right)} = .063$$

Finally, using the Z test:

$$Z = \frac{P_1 - P_2}{S_{D_p}} = \frac{.417 - .326}{.063} = \frac{.091}{.063} = 1.44$$

What is our decision regarding the null hypothesis? What is your interpretation of this finding?

There is a "catch" involved with using the Z test. The rule is that p or q, whichever is smaller, multiplied by N_1 or N_2 whichever is smaller, must result in a product > 5. For example;

The U.S. Senate has voted on the use of the determinate sentence. A total of 18.4% of the Democrats (9/49) and 4.3% of the Republicans (2/47) voted for the use of the determinate sentence. What are the research and null hypotheses?

$$P = \frac{F_1 + F_2}{N_1 + N_2} = \frac{9 + 2}{49 + 47} = \frac{11}{96} = .115$$

$$q = 1 - p = 1 - .115 = .885$$

Pooled estimate of the parameter proportion:

$$S_{D_p} = \sqrt{pq\left(\frac{1}{N_1} + \frac{1}{N_2}\right)} = \sqrt{(.115)(.885)\left(\frac{1}{49} + \frac{1}{47}\right)} = .065$$

Now before computing the Z test, the rule is that p or q, whichever is smaller, multiplied by N_1 or N_2, whichever is smaller, must result in a product > 5.

$$P \times N_2 = .115 \times 47 = 5.4$$

Thus, the rule applies to our example. When this product falls between 5 and 10, a correction for continuity must be applied by reducing the absolute value of the numerator of the Z test ($P_1 - P_2$) by the quantity .5 so:

$$.5\left(\frac{49}{(49)} + \frac{47}{(47)}\right) = .5\left(\frac{(96)}{(2303)}\right) = .5(.042) = .021$$

$$P_1 - P_2 = .184 - .042 = .141$$

The correction $= .141 - .021 = .120$

Therefore our adjusted $Z = \dfrac{P_1 - P_2}{S_{D_p}} = \dfrac{.120}{.065} = 1.85$

What is the decision regarding the H_0? How would you interpret this finding? Remember, the Z test is only appropriate when $N > 30$. If $N < 30$, the ratio you compute should be interpreted as a t test.

Example: You have observed 28 cases in a courtroom and recorded the 57.1% (4/7) of the offenders represented by private counsel and 33.3% (7/21) of the offenders represented by public defenders were released on their own recognizance (ROR).

Research Hypothesis: Offenders represented by private counsel are more likely to be released on their own recognizance than those represented by public defenders.

Null Hypothesis: Type of counsel does not have an impact upon the decision to release offenders on their own recognizance.

Pooled estimate of the parameter proportion:

$$P = \frac{F_1 + F_2}{N_1 + N_2} = \frac{4 + 7}{7 + 21} = \frac{11}{28} = .393$$

$$q = 1 - p = 1 - .393 = .607$$

Standard Error of the Proportion

$$S_{D_p} = \sqrt{pq\left(\frac{1}{N_1} + \frac{1}{N_2}\right)} = \sqrt{(.393)(.607)\left(\frac{1}{7} + \frac{1}{21}\right)} = .213$$

Then as a *t* test:

$$t = \frac{P^1 - P^2}{S_{D_p}} = \frac{.571 - .333}{.213} = \frac{.238}{.213} = 1.11$$

Degrees of freedom $= N_1 + N_2 - 2 = 28 - 2 = 26$

Using Table B, we need a *t* value of 2.06 at the .05 level. Therefore, our decision is to accept the null hypothesis and conclude that type of counsel does not have an impact upon the decision to release offenders on their own recognizance.

SUMMARY

In this chapter we learned that the *t*-distribution is one of many statistical distributions. It is similar to the normal distribution, however, its exact shape depends on the degrees of freedom. The *t* test, which is based on the *t*-distribution, examines the difference between two sample means when the sample is less than 30.

The Difference Between Proportions test is similar to the *t* test in that it can be used with very small samples. The difference is that it is used to measure the difference between two proportions, rather than two means.

In the next chapter we will investigate several statistical tests that are used by criminal justice researchers to measure relationships and to begin prediction; correlation and simple regression.

EXERCISES

For each of the following problems you must:

a. State the research and null hypotheses.
b. Check for significance at the .05 level and make a decision regarding the null hypothesis.
c. Interpret your findings and state a conclusion.

1. The governor of Florida wants a report on the effects of the death penalty. Homicide rates (per 100,000 population) in Florida cities, two weeks before and two weeks after an execution are noted below.

City	Rate Before	Rate After
Pompano Beach	23	19
Tallahassee	15	16
Tampa	12	18
Miami	20	17
Orlando	13	11

Using the above data calculate a t test.

2. Suppose we have two types of counties, one urban and one rural, and we want to compare them with respect to the percentage of persons who feel that crime is a real problem.

Urban	Rural
$N = 29$	$N = 23$
$\overline{X}_1 = 62$	$\overline{X}_2 = 47$
$\Sigma x_1^2 = 60$	$\Sigma x_2^2 = 44$

Using the above data, calculate a t test.

3. In 1927, Ohio judges used the determinate sentence. In his study, Kramer discovered that among 1,367 cases, 387/752 first offenders and 401/615 recidivists were sentenced under the 1927 statute, and thus received added time to their sentences. Using the above data, calculate a Difference Between Proportions test.

KEY TERMS

t-distribution

degrees of freedom

independent sample

nonindependent sample

t test

differences between proportions test

7

CORRELATION AND SIMPLE REGRESSION

This chapter will examine several statistical tests that allow the criminal justice researcher to study the relationship between two or more variables. As we shall see, correlation is the first step in prediction.

CORRELATION

Often, the criminal justice researcher wishes to measure the extent to which two or more variables are "related" to each other. In order to answer this question, it is necessary to determine (1) whether or not an association exists, (2) the magnitude or strength of the association, and (3) the nature of the relationship.

Correlation is a measure of relationship between two variables. It indicates the degree to which two or more variables are associated. The numerical value of measures of association, like the Pearson's Correlation Coefficient, range in value from -1.00 to $+1.00$ (perfect correlation). Note that a correlation of $+.65$ is the same size as one of $-.65$. The sign indicates the direction of the relationship, *not* the strength. When two variables are positively related, as one increases, the other increases, or as one decreases the other decreases, i.e., the number of handguns in the population, and the number of homicides. When two variables are inversely related, as one increases the other decreases, or as one decreases, the other increases, i.e., the number of beat patrolmen and the amount of crime committed. A value of .00 would indicate the absence of a relationship.

The first step in correlation is to plot a scatter diagram. This permits the researcher to examine the extent of the relationship between two variables in a preliminary and informal manner. It generally indicates whether or not there is an apparent relationship and, if there is a relationship, it may suggest whether it is linear or non-linear. If the relationship is linear, the scatter diagram will show whether the relationship is positive or negative. Figure 7.1 illustrates some of the relationships that are possible with cor-

A. Positive Relationship

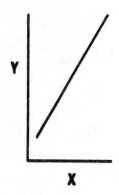

B. Negative Relationship

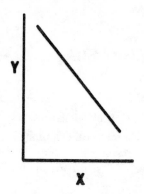

C. No Relationship

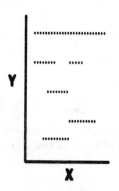

D. Curvilinear Relationship

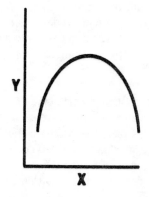

Figure 7.1. Scatter Diagrams

relation. Here, we see a perfect positive relationship in which a straight line runs from the lower left of the scatter diagram to the upper right. With the perfect negative relationship, the points fall along a straight line, running from the upper left corner of the scatter diagram to the lower right corner. We also see examples of a very weak relationship and a curvilinear relationship. The strength is generally gauged by the number of scores that group around some central direction.

The measure of association that we will examine here is the Pearson's

Product Moment Correlation, or r. There are two assumptions which underlie its use:

1. The data must be at least interval in nature.
2. The association between the two variables must be linear.

$$r = \frac{N\Sigma XY - (\Sigma X)(\Sigma Y)}{\sqrt{[N\Sigma X^2 - (\Sigma X)^2][N\Sigma Y^2 - (\Sigma Y)^2]}}$$

where N = number of pairs of values
  XY = the sum of the cross products of the paired scores
  ΣX = the sum of all values of one characteristic in the sample (independent variable)
  ΣX^2 = the sum of the squares of all values of this same characteristic in the sample
  ΣY = the sum of all values of the other characteristic in the sample (dependent variable)
  ΣY^2 = the sum of the squares of all values of this other characteristic in the sample

For example, we wish to examine whether or not there is a relationship between the unemployment rate of probationers and the unemployment rate of the county in which they reside over an eleven month period.

X = County unemployment rate (percent)
Y = Probationers unemployment rate (percent)

Month	X	Y	XY	X^2	Y^2
1	8	52	416	64	2704
2	9	59	531	81	3481
3	7	55	385	49	3025
4	11	60	660	121	3600
5	12	62	744	144	3844
6	9	49	441	81	2401
7	6	50	300	36	2500
8	7	49	343	49	2401
9	8	51	408	64	2601
10	5	46	230	25	2116
11	4	44	176	16	1936
	$\Sigma X = 86$	$\Sigma Y = 577$	$\Sigma XY = 4634$	$\Sigma X^2 = 730$	$\Sigma Y^2 = 30609$

Scatter Diagram:

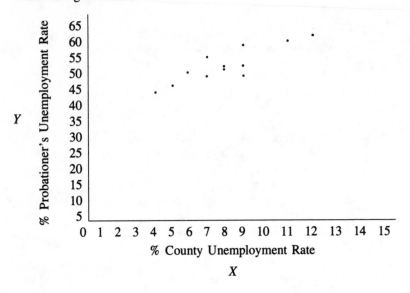

What can we say about the linearity of the relationship between these two variables?

The first step in calculating Pearson's r is to set up the preceding table. Then:

A. Pair the values of X and Y
B. Sum the values of X, ΣX
C. Sum the values of Y, ΣY
D. Multiply the two numbers in each pair, then sum the cross products, ΣXY
E. Square all values of X, then sum them, ΣX^2
F. Square all values of Y, then sum them, ΣY^2
G. $N\Sigma XY = (11)(4634) = 50974$
H. $(\Sigma X)(\Sigma Y) = (86)(577) = 49622$
I. $N\Sigma XY - (\Sigma X)(\Sigma Y) = 50974 - 49622 = 1352$

With steps A through I you have calculated the value of the numerator.

J. $N\Sigma X^2 = (11)(730) = 8030$
K. $(\Sigma X)^2 = (86)^2 = 7396$
L. $[N\Sigma X^2 - (\Sigma X)^2] = 8030 - 7396 = 634$
M. $N\Sigma Y^2 = (11)(30609) = 336699$
N. $(\Sigma Y)^2 = (577)^2 = 332929$
O. $[N\Sigma Y^2 - (\Sigma Y)^2] = 336699 - 332929 = 3770$
P. Multiply step L × step O. $634 \times 3770 = 2390180$
Q. Take the square root $\sqrt{2390180} = 1546.02$

Now with steps J through Q, you have calculated the value of the denominator of the formula.

R. $r = \dfrac{1352}{1546.02} = .8745$

Finally, using Table E, test the significance of the r. Note that you must first determine the appropriate number of degrees of freedom for correlation that is equal to the number of pairs minus 2.

The table indicates that with 9 degrees of freedom and two variables, a value of .602 is required for significance at the .05 level. Therefore, our decision would be to reject the null hypothesis, and conclude that there is a strong positive correlation between the unemployment rate for probationers and the unemployment rate for the county over an eleven month period.

INTERPRETING CORRELATION

Correlation characterizes the existence of a relationship between variables. However, it says nothing about the reasons for the existence of a relationship between the variables. It indicates only that two or more variables vary together either positively or negatively. The existence of a correlation between two variables *is not* an unfailing clue to the existence of a cause and effect relationship.

X ----------> Y could be due to Z

Often, the effect of these variables upon the original relationship is concealed. When this occurs, we have encountered a *spurious* correlation—a correlation in which hidden factors exert an effect on Y which is erroneously credited to X.

In order to interpret r we normally consider whether the obtained r is significant. Can we reject the null hypothesis of no correlation? If yes, then consider (1) What is the direction of the relationship, positive or negative? (2) What is the magnitude of the relationship? Unlike the first two steps, gauging of the magnitude of the relationship calls for the subjective judgment on the part of the researcher. Statistical significance only puts researchers in a position to interpret the magnitude of the correlation, it does not do this for them. The following is a rough guide of how the *magnitude* of r is generally interpreted. It follows for either positive or negative correlation.

< .20	slight, negligible
.20 − .40	low, definite but small
.40 − .70	moderate, substantial
.70 − .90	high, marked
> .90	very high, very dependable

Another important feature of correlation is r^2, the coefficient of determination. The r^2 expresses the proportion of the variance of Y "determined" by X, considering X as the independent and Y as the dependent variable. It also helps to interpret the magnitude of the correlation. For example, our $r = .87$, therefore, $r^2 = .76$. So, 76 percent of the variance of Y is "determined" or "explained" by X. Remember, "determined" does not mean "caused by."

Another example of a correlation technique is the Spearman Rank Correlation Coefficient, or Spearman's Rho.

SPEARMAN RANK CORRELATION COEFFICIENT

The principle behind Spearman's Rho is simple and direct. We compare the rankings of two sets of scores by taking the differences in ranks, squaring these differences and then adding them. Finally, the formula manipulates the resultant measure, through the use of constants, so that the value of rho will be $+1.0$ whenever the rankings are in perfect agreement, -1.0 if they are in perfect disagreement, and zero if there is no relationship whatsoever.

The following steps are behind the use of Spearman's Rho:

1. Rank the observations of the X variable from 1 to N. Do the same for the Y variable.
2. List the N subjects. Give each subject's rank on the X variable and on the Y variable next to the entry.
3. Determine the value of D, or the difference between the two scores for each subject by subtracting his or her rank Y from their X rank. Square this value to obtain D^2 and then sum the values to obtain ΣD^2.
4. When ties occur, each of the scores is assigned the average of the ranks which would have been assigned had no ties occurred.
5. Test for significance using Table B.

Spearman's Rho is a measure of association which requires that both variables are at least ordinal in nature so that the objects or individuals under study may be ranked in two ordered series. The difference, or D $(X - Y)$, serves as an indication of the disparity between the two sets of rankings. The magnitude of the various Ds gives us an idea of how close the relationship between the two variables is. The larger the Ds, the less perfect the association between the two variables. For example, we wish to examine the relationship between the hours of practice shooting and proficiency in marksmanship for 12 police officers.

Officer	Hours of Practice	Proficiency	Rank on	Rank on		
	X	Y	X	Y	D	D²
A	24	75	1	4	−3	9
B	23	83	2	2	0	0
C	19.5	98	3	1	2	4
D	18	80	4	3	1	1
E	17	74	5	5	0	0
F	16	69	6.5	8	−1.5	2.25
G	16	71	6.5	6	0.5	0.25
H	15	68	8	9	−1	1
I	14.5	59	9	11	−2	4
J	14	62	10.5	10	0.5	0.25
K	14	70	10.5	7	3.5	12.25
L	10	54	12	12	0	0
					$\Sigma D^2 =$	34

N = 12

$$\text{Spearman's Rho} = 1 - \frac{6\Sigma D^2}{N(N^2 - 1)} = 1 - \frac{204}{1716} = .881$$

Where 1 and 6 are constants.

This would certainly be called a high positive correlation. Of course, it remains to be seen whether it is statistically significant. To determine if this result is significant, a special kind of *t* test is calculated.

$$t = \text{rho} \sqrt{\frac{N - 2}{1 - \text{rho}^2}}$$

So, for our example

$$.881 \sqrt{\frac{12 - 2}{1 - .776}} = .881 \sqrt{\frac{10}{.224}} = 5.89$$

The degrees of freedom for Spearman's Rho is $N - 2$. Examining Table B we can see that a *t* value of 2.23 is required at the .05 level. Since the value we obtained is considerably higher, our decision would be to reject the null hypothesis. The interpretation of Spearman's Rho for all practical purposes may be done in the same fashion as Pearson's Product Moment Correlation.

The final statistical test we will examine in this chapter is simple linear regression. We should make one thing clear, "simple" does not mean that this is easy. It refers to the fact that only two variables are being tested. This is in contrast to multiple regression, which involves more than two variables.

SIMPLE LINEAR REGRESSION

Regression analysis is very closely related to correlation. In fact, the *r* used to indicate the coefficient of correlation really stands for regression. Basically, we are studying the regression of *Y* scores upon *X* scores. In other words, how do *Y* scores "go back to" or "depend upon" the *X* scores?

Regression is based on Galton's "regression toward mediocrity," a phenomenon observed in studies of inheritance. Tall parents tend to have shorter children and vice versa. The heights of the children tend to "regress" or "go back to" the mean height of the population. The emphasis here is on prediction. When we use regression analysis, we are essentially interested in the description of a predictive relationship.

If we want to predict *Y* from *X* and the correlation between *X* and *Y* is zero, the best predictor is the mean. In this situation, for any given *X* we can only predict to the mean of *Y*. The higher the correlation, the better the prediction. If $r = 1.00$, the prediction is perfect. When *r* is less than 1.00, the prediction is less accurate and "regresses" toward the mean. If *X* and *Y* values are plotted when $r = 1.00$, they will all lie on a straight line. The higher the correlation, the closer the plotted values will be to the regression line. The basic equation of simple linear regression is as follows:

$$\hat{Y} = a + bX$$

Where $\hat{Y}$ = predicted scores of the dependent variable

               X = scores of the independent variable

               a = the *Y* intercept, the point at which the regression line crosses the *Y* axis, representing the predicted value of *Y* when $X = 0$

               b = the regression coefficient, is the slope of the regression line and indicates the expected change in *Y* with a change of one unit in *X*

Again, a regression equation is a predictive formula. Y values are predicted from X values.

For example, one of the major theories in corrections is prisonization— the process of becoming a prisoner. The theory states that the longer a person is incarcerated, the more "prisonized" this person will become, and their readjustment to society will be hampered. We have decided to test the prisonization hypothesis with a random sample of inmates using a scale designed to test the degree of prisonization, where 0 equals no prisonization and 10 equals a high degree of prisonization. Thus, prisonization is our dependent variable (Y), and time served (in years) is our independent variable (X).

Prisoner	X	$x = (X - \overline{X})$	x^2	Y	$y = (Y - \overline{Y})$	y^2	xy
A	0	-3.4	11.56	1	-3.6	12.96	12.24
B	2	-1.4	1.96	3	-1.6	2.56	2.24
C	5	1.6	2.56	4	-0.6	.36	-0.96
D	4	0.6	0.36	6	1.4	1.96	0.84
E	6	2.6	6.76	9	4.4	19.36	11.44
$N=5$	$\Sigma X=17$		$\Sigma x^2=23.20$	$\Sigma Y=23$		$\Sigma y^2=37.20$	$\Sigma xy=25.80$

$$\overline{X} = 3.4 \qquad \overline{Y} = 4.6$$
$$SDx = 2.15 \qquad SDy = 2.73$$

Next, plot a scatter diagram.

The regression line is called the least-square line or the line of best fit. The term "least-squares" means that the regression line is fitted in such a way that the squared errors are, on the average, minimized. Now solve for a and b

$$b = \frac{\Sigma xy}{\Sigma x^2} = \frac{25.8}{23.2} = 1.11$$

$$a = \overline{Y} - b(\overline{X}) = 4.6 - (1.11 \times 3.4) = 4.6 - 3.874 = .826 = 0.83$$

Remember, b is the slope of the regression line, or the ratio of the change in Y corresponding to a change in X. So, in our equation, as X changes by 1, Y will change by 1.11 units. *b is used to plot our regression line, a is the y* intercept or the value of Y if $x = 0$.

$$\hat{Y} = .83 + 1.11X$$

Finally, we calculate

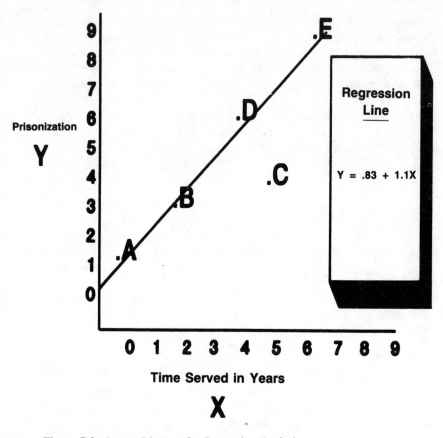

Figure 7.2. Scatter Diagram for Regression Analysis

$$r = \frac{\Sigma xy}{\sqrt{(\Sigma x^2)(\Sigma y^2)}} = \frac{25.8}{\sqrt{(23.2)(37.2)}} = \frac{25.8}{\sqrt{863.04}} = \frac{25.8}{29.4} = .88$$

The r indicates a strong positive correlation between years served in prison and prisonization. As time served increases by one year, a prisoner's score on the prisonization scale will increase by 1.11 units. To determine the errors in our prediction

Prisoner	X	Y	bX	$\hat{Y}$	$(Y - \hat{Y})$	e^2
A	0	1	0	0.83	0.17	0.03
B	2	3	2.22	3.05	−0.05	0.00
C	5	4	5.55	6.38	−2.38	5.66
D	4	6	4.44	5.27	0.73	0.53
E	6	9	6.66	7.49	1.51	2.28
						8.50

The sum of $e^2 = 8.50$. This is the total squared error. The average value across the sample $= 8.50/5 = 1.70$. This value is used in least squares, and the sum of 8.50 is used in calculating various tests of significance.

SUMMARY

Correlation is a measure of relationship between two variables. Relationships can be positive or negative and can vary in strength. Although there are about ten different statistical methods that can be used to calculate correlation, the most widely used is the Pearson Product Moment Correlation. This chapter also examined Spearman's Rho, which is used to measure the correlation of rank order. Finally, we briefly described Simple Linear Regression which is used in prediction. All of these measures of correlation are used in criminal justice research. In the next chapter we will investigate one of the most popular nonparametric statistics, chi-square.

EXERCISES

For each of the following problems:

    a. State the research and null hypothesis.
    b. Check for significance at the .05 level and make a decision regarding the null hypothesis.
    c. Interpret your findings and state a conclusion.

1. Police and Civilian Deaths, 1969-1984

Year	Number of Police Killed as a Result of Criminal Action	Number of Civilians Killed by Police
1969	90	290
1970	120	320
1971	129	409
1972	115	296
1973	134	372
1974	132	370
1975	129	330
1976	111	286
1977	93	263
1978	93	265
1979	106	301
1980	112	305
1981	118	315
1982	110	310

(problem continues next page)

1983	115	320
1984	107	310

Using the above data, calculate a Pearson's *r* and plot a scatter diagram.

2. You wish to examine the relationship between divorce rates (*X*) and the juvenile delinquency rates (*Y*) for eight communities.

Communities	Divorce Rate*	Juvenile Delinquency Rate**
1	10	8
2	17	18
3	6	6
4	25	20
5	12	20
6	18	10
7	20	14
8	4	5

*Number of divorcees per 1000 married women 15 years and over.
**Number of adjudicated delinquents per 1000 persons under 18.

Using the above data calculate a Spearman's Rho.

3. You want to determine if it is possible to predict the number of forcible rapes from 10 midsized cities based on the number of police officers in those cities.

City	Number of Forcible Rapes	Number of Police Officers
1	285	869
2	184	516
3	34	200
4	219	692
5	372	933
6	80	296
7	26	120
8	17	198
9	156	492
10	423	203

Using simple linear regression, determine whether the predictability of forcible rape rates is related to the number of police officers. Include a scatter diagram.

KEY TERMS

correlation

positive relationship

negative relationship

scatterplot

spurious relationship

simple linear regression

8

ANALYSIS OF VARIANCE:
AN INTRODUCTION

As previously demonstrated, the t test of sample means makes comparisons between two different samples. Therefore, researchers must consider other methods when they wish to make comparisons and draw inferences about three or more different samples. Of course, the researcher could determine all possible pairs of samples and then compare the t values between each possible pair of samples. However, this procedure would be tedious, confusing, and almost impossible to interpret. For example, the possible number of samples which can be compared two at a time is

$$\frac{N(N - 1)}{2}$$

where $N =$ the number of samples

If you had four samples, the number of possible comparisons would be

$$\frac{4(4 - 1)}{2}$$

or 6. Once you completed all these calculations, what could you say about the differences between the four samples?

One possible method to deal with this situation is to use analysis of variance (ANOVA). ANOVA is a method for determining the significance of the difference between any number of sample means simultaneously. There is no limit to the number of sample means that can be compared under ANOVA. For example, a researcher could compare the average burglary sentence handed down in the courtrooms of several different judges over several years. This example illustrates that ANOVA can not only compare different sample means, but can compare the scores of a single group (i.e., judges) over several points in time. Thus, you could examine if Judge Farquart was consistent in the nature of his burglary sentences over the years. ANOVA allows you to compare three or more groups, although two groups can be used. Also, the dependent variable in the analysis must be measured at the interval or ratio level.

With ANOVA, all of the data are treated at once and an overall null hypothesis between the means of the samples is the focus of the analysis. ANOVA specifically tests the null hypothesis that the sample means under consideration are equal. To test this null hypothesis, we compare the variation of the samples with the variation within the samples. The variation of sample means from the total (or grand) mean is called the between groups variance or SS_b. The average variability of the scores within each sample is called the within groups variance or SS_w. The final consideration is the total variation among all the scores combined or the total variance (SS_t).

For example, assume that we have conducted a victimization survey in four cities (Metropolis, Gotham City, Oz, and Utopia) and we wish to compare the mean rates of burglary for these cities. Here, the null hypothesis is that there is no difference in the mean burglary victimization rates among the four cities. We decide to use ANOVA and set the significance level at .05. We surveyed 100 families (selected at random) in each city.

City	ΣX	ΣX^2	N	$\overline{X}$
Metropolis	476	3414	100	4.76
Gotham City	442	3322	100	4.42
Oz	351	3629	100	3.51
Utopia	657	5413	100	6.57
TOTALS	1926	15,778	400	4.81

Using the whole score method, we first compute the total variance (SS_t)

$$SS_t = \Sigma X^2_t - \frac{(\Sigma X_t)^2}{Nt} = 15,778 - \frac{(1926)^2}{400} = 6504$$

The next step is to compute the between groups variance (SS_b)

$$SS_b = \left[\frac{(\Sigma X_t)^2}{N} \right] - \frac{(\Sigma X_t)^2}{Nt}$$

$$SS_b = \left[\frac{(476)^2}{100} + \frac{(442)^2}{100} + \frac{(351)^2}{100} + \frac{(657)^2}{100} \right] - \frac{(1926)^2}{400} = 494$$

Next, compute the within groups variance (SS_w)

$$SS_w = SS_t - SS_b = 6504 - 494 = 6010$$

Calculate the degrees of freedom for each group

Total $df_t = N_t - 1 = 400 - 1 = 399$
Between groups $df_b = N$ of groups $- 1 = 4 - 1 = 3$
Within groups $df_w = df_t - df_b = 399 - 3 = 396$

Our next step is to obtain the mean squares values (variance estimates). These mean squares are obtained by dividing each of the sum of squares by its respective number of degrees of freedom. The resulting between and within group mean squares are two estimates of the population variance.

$$MS_b = \frac{SS_b}{df_b} = \frac{494}{3} = 164.7$$

$$MS_w = \frac{SS_w}{df_w} = \frac{6010}{396} = 15.2$$

Finally, we calculate the value of F. F is a statistic which tells us whether or not the differences between the sample means are statistically significant. The greater the value of F, the more likely it is that the difference between the sample means is statistically significant.

$$F = \frac{MS_b}{MS_w} = \frac{164.6}{15.1} = 10.8$$

If we were conducting this analysis on a computer, it would provide us with an ANOVA table. This table summarizes all of the figures which we have calculated.

TABLE 8.1.   ANOVA Summary Table

Source of Variation	Sum of Squares	Degrees of Freedom	MS	F
Between Groups	494	3	164.7	10.8
Within Groups	6010	396	15.2	
Total	6504	399		

Using the F table (Table C), we see that an F value of 2.62 is required to reject the null hypothesis at the .05 level of significance. Since our F value is 10.8, we can reject the null hypothesis. Our conclusion is that the difference in the mean rates of burglary between the four cities is statistically significant.

INTERPRETING ANOVA

ANOVA is our first brush with causal analysis. One or more variables are introduced in an attempt to explain or to predict the outcome of other variables. Here, we are considering "one-way" ANOVA. In other words, we are using one independent variable (city) to explain the dependent variable (burglary victimization rates). The SS_t (total variation) has two sources. First, the SS_b (between groups variance) originates in either the differences between the samples, treatment effects, or measurement error. The second source, SS_w (within groups variance) is determined by random error within each sample.

ANOVA focuses on two independent estimates of the population variance. The MS_b (mean square between samples) is based upon the variability observed among the sample means. The assumption is that MS_b is due to either the effect of the treatment or to measurement error. The MS_w (mean square within samples) is based on the variability within samples which is mostly attributable to random error.

The F ratio is the ratio of the observed between groups variance to an estimate of that variation based upon the assumption that the null hypothesis is true. If it is true, the observed and estimated between groups variance should be about the same and the F value will be equal to one. If it is false, the observed between group variance should be greater than the estimated value and the F value should be greater than one and may even approach statistical significance, enabling the researcher to reject the null hypothesis.

ASSUMPTIONS SURROUNDING THE USE OF ANOVA

There are several assumptions which must be met before the researcher can consider the use of ANOVA. First, each element in the samples should be selected at random. Recall that the families surveyed in our example were randomly selected. The variance of the samples should be equal or homogeneous. The samples should be independent and nonrelated. Yet, ANOVA is extremely robust. This means that the homogeneity of variance requirement is often violated without damaging the integrity of the analysis. However, the sample sizes should be the same or at least very similar in size.

In our example, ANOVA tested the null hypothesis that there is no difference in the mean burglary victimization rates between the four cities. Our research hypothesis asserts that there is a significant difference due largely to Oz's very active Neighborhood Watch Program. Our analysis demonstrated that there is a significant difference between the mean burglary victimization rates. However, we are unable to determine where the difference originates. It does not specify which of the sample means is responsible for this conclusion. Certain tests may be used with ANOVA to perform this task, but since this is a basic statistics text, we will not consider these tests here.

EXERCISES

Directions: Analyze the following problems using analysis of variance. For each question, take the following steps, using the whole score method:

(a) State your research and null hypotheses
(b) Calculate the proper figures and construct an ANOVA table
(c) Compute the F value. Check for significance at the .05 level
(d) Briefly state your conclusions

1. Suppose you wish to determine if the regions of the country differ with regard to the mean rate of homicide victimization per 100,000 population.

Region	ΣX	ΣX^2	N	$\overline{X}$
Northeast	39.8	235.38	9	4.42
North Central	65.3	476.45	12	5.44
Southern	122.1	1322.05	12	10.18
Western	94.6	882.58	12	7.88

2. You have collected self report delinquency data from three different high schools to determine if there are differences in the mean rate of delinquency among the schools. The schools are primarily attended by students from the upper (Preppie High), middle (Your Honor High) and lower (Stillis High) classes. Analyze these data through the use of ANOVA.

High School	ΣX	ΣX^2	N	$\overline{X}$
Preppie High	192	3134	12	16
Your Honor High	285	5485	15	19
Stillis High	308	6812	14	22

KEY TERMS

between groups variance (SS_b)

within groups variance (SS_w)

total variance (SS_t)

mean square

F statistic

robust

REFERENCES

ELZEY, F. (1985) *Introductory statistics: A microcomputer approach.* Belmont, CA: Brooks/Cole.
HY, R. J., D. G. FEIG, and R. M. REGOLI (1983) *Research methods and statistics: A primer for criminal justice & related sciences.* Cincinnati: Anderson.

9

CHI-SQUARE AND
MEASURES OF ASSOCIATION

One of the most widely used statistical tests is chi-square. It is an extremely popular statistic because it has very few assumptions. It is a nonparametric statistic that allows the researcher to calculate statistical significance with nominal level data. This statistic tells us whether our observations differ significantly from what would be expected by chance. "Chance" is defined in a particular way.

Chi-square is a "goodness of fit" statistic. Goodness of fit refers to a statistical evaluation of the difference between our sample observations and some distribution of observations provided by our hypothesized model of expected values at a given level of significance. It is a test of significance for nominal data. Data should be discrete and expressed in frequencies in the form of a contingency table.

SINGLE SAMPLE CHI-SQUARE

Consider the following example. A police academy is interested in admitting an equal number of males and females.

H_0: The number of males admitted is equal to the number of females admitted. H_1: More males are admitted.

The distribution (observed) is:

Male	15
Female	25
Total	40

Under H_0, our expected distribution is:

Male	20	(50%)
Female	20	(50%)
Total	40	

$$X^2 = \sum \frac{(|O_1 - E_1| - .5)^2}{E}$$

Where

O = Observed frequency.
E = Expected frequency.
$-.5$ = Yates correction for continuity.

(Note: Yates correction for continuity should only be used when the degrees of freedom = 1 or when one of the expected cell frequencies is less than 10.)

Calculations:

	O	E	$(\|O_1 - E_1\| - .5)$	$(\|O_1 - E_1\| - .5)^2$	Divided by E
Male	15	20	4.5	20.25	1.01
Female	25	20	4.5	20.25	1.01
				Σ =	2.02

To determine the degrees of freedom, df = $K - 1$, where K = the number of categories. Here df = $2 - 1 = 1$.

Using Table D, we see that our decision at the .05 level would be to accept the H_0; An equal number of males and females were admitted.

CHI-SQUARE FOR TWO INDEPENDENT SAMPLES

Often, we are interested in determining whether or not our observations are significantly different from what we would expect according to chance.

Suppose we would like to know whether significant differences exist between male and female parolees and whether or not they have been arrested while under supervision.

Relationship Between Gender and Arrest for 200 Parolees

		Gender		
		Male	Female	
Arrested	Yes	A 75	B 40	Total 115
	No	C 25	D 60	85
	Total	100	100	

H_0: There is no difference in the arrest rate between male and female
parolees

H_1: Males are more likely to be arrested while on parole than females.

First, it is necessary to calculate the expected frequency (E) for each cell.

$$E = \frac{(N \text{ row})(N \text{ column})}{N \text{ Total}}$$

$$\text{Cell A} = \frac{(115)(100)}{200} = 57.5$$

$$\text{Cell B} = \frac{(115)(100)}{200} = 57.5$$

$$\text{Cell C} = \frac{(85)(100)}{200} = 42.5$$

$$\text{Cell D} = \frac{(85)(100)}{200} = 42.5$$

Next, calculate the value of chi-square

Cell	O	E	$(\mid O_1 - E_1 \mid - .5)$	$(\mid O_1 - E_1 \mid - .5)^2$	Divided by E
A	75	57.5	17	289	5.03
B	40	57.5	17	289	5.03
C	25	42.5	17	289	6.80
D	60	42.5	17	289	6.80
					$\Sigma = 23.66$

Next, determine if the chi-square value is statistically significant. With two
independent samples, degrees of freedom = (rows − 1)(columns − 1).
For this example our degrees of freedom = $(2 - 1)(2 - 1) = 1$.

As we can see from Table D, an X^2 of 3.84 is required to reject the null
hypothesis. Since our obtained value (23.66) was greater than 3.84, we reject the null, and conclude that there was a difference in the rate of incarcera-
tion for male and female parolees. In order fully to interpret the chi-square
value we must inspect the data, since chi-square does not indicate direction. We can see from these data that male parolees were more likely to
be arrested than female parolees. This is an important point to remember,

since if the exact same numbers were simply reversed we would have obtained the same chi-square value, but our interpretation would have been completely reversed.

Assumptions behind the use of chi-square are (1) the sample of observations must be independent, (2) data can exist at any level of measurement, and (3) no cell should have an expected frequency of less than 5. When chi-square is computed and the expected cell frequencies drop below 5, the resulting value is meaningless.

One of the reasons why chi-square is so popular is the absence of restrictions on its use. The only disadvantage is the smaller the sample, the more distorted the chi-square value is likely to be. Distortion is introduced when any expected frequency is less than 5. The resulting chi-square value becomes an overestimate of the "way things are." The researcher should beware of small samples with the chi-square.

MEASURES OF ASSOCIATION FOR NOMINAL AND ORDINAL DATA

Up to this point, we have been interested in whether or not a relationship exists between variables. Three measures of association, the contingency coefficient, the phi coefficient and the Cramér's statistic are often utilized with chi-square to measure the magnitude and nature of a relationship.

Contingency Coefficient

The contingency coefficient (C) is a measure of association for use with nominal level data. It can be used with data which has been divided into more than two categories.

$$C = \sqrt{\frac{X^2}{N + X^2}} = \sqrt{\frac{23.66}{200 + 23.66}} = \sqrt{.105} = .32$$

Unlike the correlation coefficients, C does not have $+$ or $-$ 1.00 as its lower and upper limits. With an equal number of columns and rows, the upper limit of C is equal to

$$\sqrt{\frac{(K - 1)}{K}}$$

where $K =$ the number of rows.

With an unequal number of columns and rows, the upper limit follows that of the smaller number. C has no sign, so you must determine the direction and nature of the relationship by inspecting the contingency table. The major advantage of C is that there are no assumptions regarding the population distribution. It can be applied to data which are normal, skewed, continuous, discrete, nominal, ordinal, etc. Remember, if the chi-square value is statistically significant, so is the value of C.

Cramér's Statistic

Cramér's statistic is very similar to C, except that is has an upper limit of 1.

$$\text{Cramér's Statistic} = \sqrt{\frac{X^2}{N(L - 1)}}$$

where L is the smaller of either the number of columns or rows.

So, using our data from above

$$\sqrt{\frac{23.66}{200(2 - 1)}} = \sqrt{\frac{23.66}{200}} = .343$$

Phi Coefficient

The Phi coefficient is only used when data are dichotomized. If the data is divided in any other fashion, the use of C is more appropriate.

$$\text{Phi} = \sqrt{\frac{X^2}{N}} = \sqrt{\frac{23.66}{200}} = .34$$

Again, if the value of chi-square is significant, so is the value of Phi.

To evaluate the magnitude of the association, compare the computed Phi with the maximum value of Phi for this type of split. To set the maximum value, make the cell with the lowest frequency equal to zero and then compare this value to your computed Phi value. Remember, you should use C or Cramér's statistics if you do not have a 2 × 2 table.

RULES FOR THE CONSTRUCTION OF CONTINGENCY TABLES

Because contingency tables contain so much vital information, tables should meet certain standards.

(1) Tables should be fully labeled. The title should contain enough information

so that the reader is able to determine just exactly what relationship is being portrayed.

(2) The categories and content of each variable should be clearly presented so that they are not confused with one another.

(3) Usually, the independent variable (X) is on the top of the table and the dependent variable (Y) is on the side.

(4) The table should be drawn neatly and the labels should indicate what data are presented in each cell.

(5) If percentages are used, they must be clearly explained according to how they are computed. In some cases, you would present the row percentages, while in others, the column percentages would be more significant. It all depends upon the relationship that has the greatest importance in the study.

(6) Any missing cases must be clearly explained. If your sample size is 200, but your contingency table contains 195 cases, you should tell the reader that 5 cases are missing and, if possible, why the data are missing.

(7) The results of the statistical chi-square analysis should be clearly presented and at the bottom of the table.

The text of your study should discuss the conclusions, meaning and significance of the results. Refer directly to each table as you discuss its contents. If you follow these simple rules you should have clear, concise tables, which will allow the reader to easily understand the data you are presenting and the relationship it contains.

SUMMARY

The chi-square is one of the most popular nonparametric statistics. The absence of assumptions and restrictions surrounding its use make it a very useful statistic. As a "goodness of fit" statistic, chi-square allows the researcher to compare what is obtained or observed, with what is expected. In addition, the measure of association allow us to determine the strength of the relationship obtained by the chi-square.

EXERCISES

1. A criminologist investigated the relationship between new prisoners' adjustment to prison and the density of their home towns (according to whether it was urban, suburban, or rural). She assumed that prisoners from denser areas would make a better adjustment.

    a. State the research and null hypothesis
    b. Using the following data calculate a chi-square

		Home Town		
		Urban	Suburban	Rural
Adjustment to Prison	Good	85	65	17
	Bad	40	36	55

c. Calculate the Contingency Coefficient.

d. Using the alpha level of .05, state the decision that should be made with respect to the null hypothesis, and interpret the findings.

KEY TERMS

chi-square

goodness of fit

Yate's correction

measures of association

Cramér's statistic

Phi

APPENDIX

REFERENCE TABLES

TABLE A   Areas Under the Normal Curve

Z	.00	.01	.02	.03	.04	.05	.06	.07	.08	.09
0.0	0000	0040	0080	0120	0160	0199	0239	0279	0319	0359
0.1	0398	0438	0478	0517	0557	0596	0636	0675	0714	0753
0.2	0793	0832	0871	0910	0948	0987	1026	1064	1103	1141
0.3	1179	1217	1255	1293	1331	1368	1406	1443	1480	1517
0.4	1554	1591	1628	1664	1700	1736	1772	1808	1844	1879
0.5	1915	1950	1985	2019	2054	2088	2123	2157	2190	2224
0.6	2257	2291	2324	2357	2389	2422	2454	2486	2517	2549
0.7	2580	2611	2642	2673	2704	2734	2764	2794	2823	2852
0.8	2881	2910	2939	2967	2995	3023	3051	3078	3106	3133
0.9	3159	3186	3212	3238	3264	3289	3315	3340	3365	3389
1.0	3413	3438	3461	3485	3508	3531	3554	3577	3599	3621
1.1	3643	3665	3686	3708	3729	3749	3770	3790	3810	3830
1.2	3849	3869	3888	3907	3925	3944	3962	3980	3997	4015
1.3	4032	4049	4066	4082	4099	4115	4131	4147	4162	4177
1.4	4192	4207	4222	4236	4251	4265	4279	4292	4306	4319
1.5	4332	4345	4357	4370	4382	4394	4406	4418	4429	4441
1.6	4452	4463	4474	4484	4495	4505	4515	4525	4535	4545
1.7	4554	4564	4573	4582	4591	4599	4608	4616	4625	4633
1.8	4641	4649	4656	4664	4671	4678	4686	4693	4699	4706
1.9	4713	4719	4726	4732	4738	4744	4750	4756	4761	4767
2.0	4772	4778	4783	4788	4793	4798	4803	4808	4812	4817
2.1	4821	4826	4830	4834	4838	4842	4846	4850	4854	4857
2.2	4861	4864	4868	4871	4875	4878	4881	4884	4887	4890
2.3	4893	4896	4898	4901	4904	4906	4909	4911	4913	4916
2.4	4918	4920	4922	4925	4927	4929	4931	4932	4934	4936
2.5	4938	4940	4941	4943	4945	4946	4948	4949	4951	4952
2.6	4953	4955	4956	4957	4959	4960	4961	4962	4963	4964
2.7	4965	4966	4967	4968	4969	4970	4971	4972	4973	4974
2.8	4974	4975	4976	4977	4977	4978	4979	4979	4980	4981
2.9	4981	4982	4982	4983	4984	4984	4985	4985	4986	4986
3.0	4987	4987	4987	4988	4988	4989	4989	4989	4990	4990
3.1	4990	4991	4991	4991	4992	4992	4992	4992	4993	4993
3.2	4993	4993	4994	4994	4994	4994	4994	4995	4995	4995
3.3	4995	4995	4995	4996	4996	4996	4996	4996	4996	4997
3.4	4997	4997	4997	4997	4997	4997	4997	4997	4997	4998
3.5	4998	4998	4998	4998	4998	4998	4998	4998	4998	4998
3.6	4998	4998	4999	4999	4999	4999	4999	4999	4999	4999
3.7	4999	4999	4999	4999	4999	4999	4999	4999	4999	4999
3.8	499928									
3.9	499952									
4.0	499968									
4.5	499997									
5.0	500000									

SOURCE: W. Usui, University of Louisville. Used with permission.

TABLE B   Distribution of *t*

Degrees of freedom	One-Tail Significance			
	.10	.05	.025	.01
1	3.08	6.31	12.69	31.67
2	1.89	2.92	4.30	6.95
3	1.64	2.35	3.18	4.54
4	1.53	2.13	2.78	3.75
5	1.48	2.02	2.57	3.36
6	1.44	1.94	2.45	3.14
7	1.42	1.89	2.36	3.00
8	1.40	1.86	2.30	2.89
9	1.38	1.83	2.26	2.82
10	1.37	1.81	2.23	2.76
11	1.36	1.80	2.20	2.72
12	1.36	1.78	2.18	2.68
13	1.35	1.77	2.16	2.65
14	1.34	1.76	2.14	2.62
15	1.34	1.75	2.13	2.60
16	1.34	1.75	2.12	2.58
17	1.33	1.74	2.11	2.56
18	1.33	1.73	2.10	2.55
19	1.33	1.73	2.09	2.54
20	1.33	1.72	2.09	2.53
21	1.32	1.72	2.08	2.52
22	1.32	1.72	2.07	2.51
23	1.32	1.71	2.07	2.50
24	1.32	1.71	2.06	2.49
25	1.32	1.71	2.06	2.48
26	1.31	1.71	2.06	2.48
27	1.31	1.70	2.05	2.47
28	1.31	1.70	2.05	2.47
29	1.31	1.70	2.05	2.46
30	1.31	1.70	2.04	2.46
31	1.31	1.70	2.04	2.45
32	1.31	1.69	2.04	2.45
33	1.31	1.69	2.03	2.44
34	1.31	1.69	2.03	2.44
35	1.31	1.69	2.03	2.44
40	1.30	1.68	2.02	2.42
45	1.30	1.68	2.01	2.41
50	1.30	1.68	2.01	2.40
60	1.30	1.67	2.00	2.39
70	1.29	1.67	1.99	2.38
100	1.29	1.66	1.98	2.36
10000	1.28	1.64	1.96	2.33

SOURCE: W. Usui, University of Louisville. Used with permission.

NOTE: With a two-tailed test, the .025 column is used.

Reject the null hypothesis when the *t* value is equal to or greater than that listed in the table.

TABLE C   Table of F

Degrees of Freedom Between Groups (top value = .05 level, bottom value = .01 level)

df within	1	2	3	4	5	6	7	8	9	10	11	12	14	16	20	24	30	40	50	75	100	200	500	∞
1	161 / 4,052	200 / 4,999	216 / 5,403	225 / 5,625	230 / 5,764	234 / 5,859	237 / 5,928	239 / 5,981	241 / 6,022	242 / 6,056	243 / 6,082	244 / 6,106	245 / 6,142	246 / 6,169	248 / 6,208	249 / 6,234	250 / 6,258	251 / 6,286	252 / 6,302	253 / 6,323	253 / 6,334	254 / 6,352	254 / 6,361	254 / 6,366
2	18.51 / 98.49	19.00 / 99.01	19.16 / 99.17	19.25 / 99.25	19.30 / 99.30	19.33 / 99.33	19.36 / 99.34	19.37 / 99.36	19.38 / 99.38	19.39 / 99.40	19.40 / 99.41	19.41 / 99.42	19.42 / 99.43	19.43 / 99.44	19.44 / 99.45	19.45 / 99.46	19.46 / 99.47	19.47 / 99.48	19.47 / 99.48	19.48 / 99.49	19.49 / 99.49	19.49 / 99.49	19.50 / 99.50	19.50 / 99.50
3	10.13 / 34.12	9.55 / 30.81	9.28 / 29.46	9.12 / 28.71	9.01 / 28.24	8.94 / 27.91	8.88 / 27.67	8.84 / 27.49	8.81 / 27.34	8.78 / 27.23	8.76 / 27.13	8.74 / 27.05	8.71 / 26.92	8.69 / 26.83	8.66 / 26.69	8.64 / 26.60	8.62 / 26.50	8.60 / 26.41	8.58 / 36.35	8.57 / 26.23	8.56 / 26.23	8.54 / 26.18	8.54 / 26.14	8.53 / 26.12
4	7.71 / 21.20	6.94 / 18.00	6.59 / 16.69	6.39 / 15.98	6.26 / 15.52	6.16 / 15.21	6.09 / 14.98	6.04 / 14.80	6.00 / 14.66	5.96 / 14.54	5.93 / 14.45	5.91 / 14.37	5.87 / 14.24	5.84 / 14.15	5.80 / 14.02	5.77 / 13.93	5.74 / 13.83	5.71 / 13.74	5.70 / 13.69	5.68 / 13.61	5.66 / 13.57	5.65 / 13.52	5.64 / 13.48	5.63 / 13.46
5	6.61 / 16.26	5.79 / 13.27	5.41 / 12.06	5.19 / 11.39	5.05 / 10.97	4.95 / 10.67	4.88 / 10.45	4.82 / 10.27	4.78 / 10.15	4.74 / 10.05	4.70 / 9.96	4.68 / 9.89	4.64 / 9.77	4.60 / 9.68	4.56 / 9.55	4.53 / 9.47	4.50 / 9.38	4.46 / 9.29	4.44 / 9.24	4.42 / 9.17	4.40 / 9.13	4.38 / 9.07	4.37 / 9.04	4.36 / 9.02
6	5.99 / 13.74	5.14 / 10.92	4.76 / 9.78	4.53 / 9.15	4.39 / 8.75	4.28 / 8.47	4.21 / 8.26	4.15 / 8.10	4.10 / 7.98	4.06 / 7.87	4.03 / 7.79	4.00 / 7.72	3.96 / 7.60	3.92 / 7.52	3.87 / 7.39	3.84 / 7.31	3.81 / 7.23	3.77 / 7.14	3.75 / 7.09	3.72 / 7.02	3.71 / 6.99	3.69 / 6.94	3.68 / 6.90	3.67 / 6.88
7	5.59 / 12.25	4.74 / 9.55	4.35 / 8.45	4.12 / 7.85	3.97 / 7.46	3.87 / 7.19	3.79 / 7.00	3.73 / 6.84	3.68 / 6.71	3.63 / 6.62	3.60 / 6.54	3.57 / 6.47	3.52 / 6.35	3.49 / 6.27	3.44 / 6.15	3.41 / 6.07	3.38 / 5.98	3.34 / 5.90	3.32 / 5.85	3.29 / 5.78	3.28 / 5.75	3.25 / 5.70	3.24 / 5.67	3.23 / 5.65
8	5.32 / 11.26	4.46 / 8.65	4.07 / 7.59	3.84 / 7.01	3.69 / 6.63	3.58 / 6.37	3.50 / 6.19	3.44 / 6.03	3.39 / 5.91	3.34 / 5.82	3.31 / 5.74	3.28 / 5.67	3.23 / 5.56	3.20 / 5.48	3.15 / 5.36	3.12 / 5.28	3.08 / 5.20	3.05 / 5.11	3.03 / 5.06	3.00 / 5.00	2.98 / 4.96	2.96 / 4.91	2.94 / 4.88	2.93 / 4.86
9	5.12 / 10.56	4.26 / 8.02	3.86 / 6.99	3.63 / 6.42	3.48 / 6.06	3.37 / 5.80	3.29 / 5.62	3.23 / 5.47	3.18 / 5.35	3.13 / 5.26	3.10 / 5.18	3.07 / 5.11	3.02 / 5.00	2.98 / 4.92	2.93 / 4.80	2.90 / 4.73	2.86 / 4.64	2.82 / 4.56	2.80 / 4.51	2.77 / 4.45	2.76 / 4.41	2.73 / 4.36	2.72 / 4.33	2.71 / 4.31
10	4.96 / 10.04	4.10 / 7.56	3.71 / 6.55	3.48 / 5.99	3.33 / 5.64	3.22 / 5.39	3.14 / 5.21	3.07 / 5.06	3.02 / 4.95	2.97 / 4.85	2.94 / 4.78	2.91 / 4.71	2.86 / 4.60	2.82 / 4.52	2.77 / 4.41	2.74 / 4.33	2.70 / 4.25	2.67 / 4.17	2.64 / 4.12	2.61 / 4.05	2.59 / 4.01	2.56 / 3.96	2.55 / 3.93	2.54 / 3.91
11	4.84 / 9.65	3.98 / 7.20	3.59 / 6.22	3.36 / 5.67	3.20 / 5.32	3.09 / 5.07	3.01 / 4.88	2.95 / 4.74	2.90 / 4.63	2.86 / 4.54	2.82 / 4.46	2.79 / 4.40	2.74 / 4.29	2.70 / 4.21	2.65 / 4.10	2.61 / 4.02	2.57 / 3.94	2.53 / 3.86	2.50 / 3.80	2.47 / 3.74	2.45 / 3.70	2.42 / 3.66	2.41 / 3.62	2.40 / 3.60
12	4.75 / 9.33	3.88 / 6.93	3.49 / 5.95	3.26 / 5.41	3.11 / 5.06	3.00 / 4.82	2.92 / 4.65	2.85 / 4.50	2.80 / 4.39	2.76 / 4.30	2.72 / 4.22	2.69 / 4.16	2.64 / 4.05	2.60 / 3.98	2.54 / 3.86	2.50 / 3.78	2.46 / 3.70	2.42 / 3.61	2.40 / 3.56	2.36 / 3.49	2.35 / 3.46	2.32 / 3.41	2.31 / 3.38	2.30 / 3.36
14	4.60 / 8.40	3.74 / 6.11	3.34 / 5.18	3.11 / 4.67	2.96 / 4.34	2.85 / 4.10	2.77 / 3.93	2.70 / 3.79	2.65 / 3.68	2.60 / 3.59	2.56 / 3.52	2.53 / 3.45	2.48 / 3.35	2.44 / 3.27	2.39 / 3.16	2.35 / 3.08	2.31 / 3.00	2.27 / 2.92	2.24 / 2.86	2.21 / 2.79	2.19 / 2.76	2.16 / 2.70	2.14 / 2.67	2.13 / 2.65

Degree of Freedom Within Groups

Critical Values of F — Degrees of Freedom Between Groups (columns) × Degrees of Freedom Within Groups (rows). In each cell the upper value is the .05 level and the lower (bold) value is the .01 level.

Within ↓ \ Between →	1	2	3	4	5	6	7	8	9	10	11	12	14	16	20	24	30	40	50	70	100	200	400	∞
16	4.45 / **8.40**	3.59 / **6.11**	3.20 / **5.18**	2.96 / **4.67**	2.81 / **4.34**	2.70 / **4.10**	2.62 / **3.93**	2.55 / **3.79**	2.50 / **3.68**	2.45 / **3.59**	2.41 / **3.52**	2.38 / **3.45**	2.33 / **3.35**	2.29 / **3.27**	2.23 / **3.16**	2.19 / **3.08**	2.15 / **3.00**	2.11 / **2.92**	2.08 / **2.86**	2.04 / **2.79**	2.02 / **2.76**	1.99 / **2.70**	1.97 / **2.67**	1.96 / **2.65**
20	4.35 / **8.10**	3.49 / **5.85**	3.10 / **4.94**	2.87 / **4.43**	2.71 / **4.10**	2.60 / **3.87**	2.52 / **3.71**	2.45 / **3.56**	2.40 / **3.45**	2.35 / **3.37**	2.31 / **3.30**	2.28 / **3.23**	2.23 / **3.13**	2.18 / **3.05**	2.12 / **2.94**	2.08 / **2.86**	2.04 / **2.77**	1.99 / **2.69**	1.96 / **2.63**	1.92 / **2.56**	1.90 / **2.53**	1.87 / **2.47**	1.85 / **2.44**	1.84 / **2.42**
24	4.26 / **7.82**	3.40 / **5.61**	3.01 / **4.72**	2.78 / **4.22**	2.62 / **3.90**	2.51 / **3.67**	2.43 / **3.50**	2.36 / **3.36**	2.30 / **3.25**	2.26 / **3.17**	2.22 / **3.09**	2.18 / **3.03**	2.13 / **2.93**	2.09 / **2.85**	2.02 / **2.74**	1.98 / **2.66**	1.94 / **2.58**	1.89 / **2.49**	1.86 / **2.44**	1.82 / **2.36**	1.80 / **2.33**	1.76 / **2.27**	1.74 / **2.23**	1.73 / **2.21**
30	4.17 / **7.56**	3.32 / **5.39**	2.92 / **4.51**	2.69 / **4.02**	2.53 / **3.70**	2.42 / **3.47**	2.34 / **3.30**	2.27 / **3.17**	2.21 / **3.06**	2.16 / **2.98**	2.12 / **2.90**	2.09 / **2.84**	2.04 / **2.74**	1.99 / **2.66**	1.93 / **2.55**	1.89 / **2.47**	1.84 / **2.38**	1.79 / **2.29**	1.76 / **2.24**	1.72 / **2.16**	1.69 / **2.13**	1.66 / **2.07**	1.64 / **2.03**	1.62 / **2.01**
40	4.08 / **7.31**	3.23 / **5.18**	2.84 / **4.31**	2.61 / **3.83**	2.45 / **3.51**	2.34 / **3.29**	2.25 / **3.12**	2.18 / **2.99**	2.12 / **2.88**	2.07 / **2.80**	2.04 / **2.73**	2.00 / **2.66**	1.95 / **2.56**	1.90 / **2.49**	1.84 / **2.37**	1.79 / **2.29**	1.74 / **2.20**	1.69 / **2.11**	1.66 / **2.05**	1.61 / **1.97**	1.59 / **1.94**	1.55 / **1.88**	1.53 / **1.84**	1.51 / **1.81**
50	4.03 / **7.17**	3.18 / **5.06**	2.79 / **4.20**	2.56 / **3.72**	2.40 / **3.41**	2.29 / **3.18**	2.20 / **3.02**	2.13 / **2.89**	2.07 / **2.78**	2.02 / **2.70**	1.98 / **2.62**	1.90 / **2.56**	1.95 / **2.46**	1.90 / **2.39**	1.85 / **2.26**	1.78 / **2.18**	1.74 / **2.10**	1.69 / **2.00**	1.63 / **1.94**	1.55 / **1.86**	1.52 / **1.82**	1.48 / **1.76**	1.46 / **1.71**	1.44 / **1.68**
70	3.98 / **7.01**	3.13 / **4.92**	2.74 / **4.08**	2.50 / **3.60**	2.35 / **3.29**	2.23 / **3.07**	2.14 / **2.91**	2.07 / **2.77**	2.01 / **2.67**	1.97 / **2.59**	1.93 / **2.51**	1.89 / **2.45**	1.84 / **2.35**	1.79 / **2.28**	1.72 / **2.15**	1.67 / **2.07**	1.62 / **1.98**	1.56 / **1.88**	1.53 / **1.82**	1.47 / **1.74**	1.45 / **1.69**	1.40 / **1.62**	1.37 / **1.56**	1.35 / **1.53**
100	3.94 / **6.90**	3.09 / **4.82**	2.70 / **3.98**	2.46 / **3.51**	2.30 / **3.20**	2.19 / **2.99**	2.10 / **2.82**	2.03 / **2.69**	1.97 / **2.59**	1.92 / **2.51**	1.88 / **2.43**	1.85 / **2.36**	1.79 / **2.26**	1.75 / **2.19**	1.68 / **2.06**	1.63 / **1.98**	1.57 / **1.89**	1.51 / **1.79**	1.48 / **1.73**	1.42 / **1.64**	1.39 / **1.59**	1.34 / **1.51**	1.30 / **1.46**	1.28 / **1.43**
150	3.91 / **6.81**	3.06 / **4.75**	2.67 / **3.91**	2.43 / **3.44**	2.27 / **3.14**	2.16 / **2.92**	2.07 / **2.76**	2.00 / **2.62**	1.94 / **2.53**	1.89 / **2.44**	1.85 / **2.37**	1.82 / **2.30**	1.76 / **2.20**	1.71 / **2.12**	1.64 / **2.00**	1.59 / **1.91**	1.54 / **1.83**	1.47 / **1.72**	1.44 / **1.66**	1.37 / **1.56**	1.34 / **1.51**	1.29 / **1.43**	1.25 / **1.37**	1.22 / **1.33**
200	3.89 / **6.76**	3.04 / **4.71**	2.65 / **3.88**	2.41 / **3.41**	2.26 / **3.11**	2.14 / **2.90**	2.05 / **2.73**	1.98 / **2.60**	1.92 / **2.50**	1.87 / **2.41**	1.83 / **2.34**	1.80 / **2.28**	1.74 / **2.17**	1.69 / **2.09**	1.62 / **1.97**	1.57 / **1.88**	1.52 / **1.79**	1.45 / **1.69**	1.42 / **1.62**	1.35 / **1.53**	1.32 / **1.48**	1.26 / **1.39**	1.22 / **1.33**	1.19 / **1.28**
400	3.86 / **6.70**	3.02 / **4.66**	2.62 / **3.83**	2.39 / **3.36**	2.23 / **3.06**	2.12 / **2.85**	2.03 / **2.69**	1.96 / **2.55**	1.90 / **2.46**	1.85 / **2.37**	1.81 / **2.29**	1.78 / **2.23**	1.72 / **2.12**	1.67 / **2.04**	1.60 / **1.92**	1.54 / **1.84**	1.49 / **1.74**	1.42 / **1.64**	1.38 / **1.57**	1.32 / **1.47**	1.28 / **1.42**	1.22 / **1.32**	1.16 / **1.24**	1.13 / **1.19**
1,000	3.85 / **6.66**	3.00 / **4.62**	2.61 / **3.80**	2.38 / **3.34**	2.22 / **3.04**	2.10 / **2.82**	2.02 / **2.66**	1.95 / **2.53**	1.89 / **2.43**	1.84 / **2.34**	1.80 / **2.26**	1.76 / **2.20**	1.70 / **2.09**	1.65 / **2.01**	1.58 / **1.89**	1.53 / **1.81**	1.47 / **1.71**	1.41 / **1.61**	1.36 / **1.54**	1.30 / **1.44**	1.26 / **1.38**	1.19 / **1.28**	1.13 / **1.19**	1.08 / **1.11**
∞	3.84 / **6.64**	2.99 / **4.60**	2.60 / **3.78**	2.37 / **3.32**	2.21 / **3.02**	2.09 / **2.80**	2.01 / **2.64**	1.94 / **2.51**	1.88 / **2.41**	1.83 / **2.32**	1.79 / **2.24**	1.75 / **2.18**	1.69 / **2.07**	1.64 / **1.99**	1.57 / **1.87**	1.52 / **1.79**	1.46 / **1.69**	1.40 / **1.59**	1.35 / **1.52**	1.28 / **1.41**	1.24 / **1.36**	1.17 / **1.25**	1.11 / **1.15**	1.00 / **1.00**

Degrees of Freedom Within Groups

SOURCE: Besag and Besag (1985). *Statistics for the Helping Professions.* Sage. Used with permission.
NOTE: Reject the null hypothesis if the F ratio value is equal to or greater than that listed in the table.

TABLE D   Critical Values for the Chi-Square Distribution

df	.100	.050	.025	.010
1	2.706	3.842	5.024	6.637
2	4.605	5.992	7.378	9.212
3	6.252	7.815	9.349	11.347
4	7.780	9.488	11.144	13.279
5	9.237	11.071	12.834	15.089
6	10.645	12.592	14.450	16.814
7	12.017	14.068	16.014	18.478
8	13.362	15.508	17.536	20.093
9	14.684	16.920	19.024	21.669
10	15.988	18.308	20.484	23.212
11	17.275	19.676	21.921	24.728
12	18.550	21.027	23.338	26.220
13	19.812	22.363	24.737	27.691
14	21.064	23.686	26.120	29.144
15	22.308	24.996	27.490	30.581
16	23.542	26.297	28.847	32.003
17	24.769	27.588	30.192	33.412
18	25.990	28.870	31.528	34.809
19	27.204	30.144	32.854	36.194
20	28.412	31.411	34.171	37.570
21	29.616	32.671	35.480	38.936
22	30.814	33.925	36.782	40.293
23	32.007	35.173	38.077	41.642
24	33.197	36.416	39.366	42.984
25	34.382	37.653	40.648	44.318

SOURCE: W. Usui, University of Louisville. Used with permission.
NOTE: Reject the null hypothesis if the chi-square value is equal to or greater than that listed
in the table.

TABLE E   Table of 5% and 1% Points for *r* and *R*

Degrees of Freedom	Number of Variables				Degrees of Freedom	Number of Variables			
	2	3	4	5		2	3	4	5
1	.997	.999	.999	.999	24	.388	.470	.523	.562
	1.000	1.000	1.000	1.000		.496	.565	.609	.642
2	.950	.975	.983	.987	25	.381	.462	.514	.553
	.990	.995	.997	.998		.487	.555	.600	.633
3	.878	.930	.950	.961	26	.374	.454	.506	.545
	.959	.976	.983	.987		.478	.546	.590	.624
4	.811	.881	.912	.930	27	.367	.446	.498	.536
	.917	.949	.962	.970		.470	.538	.582	.615
5	.754	.836	.874	.898	28	.361	.439	.490	.529
	.874	.917	.937	.949		.463	.530	.573	.606
6	.707	.795	.839	.867	29	.355	.432	.482	.521
	.834	.886	.911	.927		.456	.522	.565	.598
7	.666	.758	.807	.838	30	.349	.426	.476	.514
	.798	.855	.885	.904		.449	.514	.558	.591
8	.632	.726	.777	.811	35	.325	.397	.445	.482
	.765	.827	.860	.882		.418	.481	.523	.556
9	.602	.697	.750	.786	40	.304	.373	.419	.455
	.735	.800	.836	.861		.393	.454	.494	.526
10	.576	.671	.726	.763	45	.288	.353	.397	.432
	.708	.776	.814	.840		.372	.430	.470	.501
11	.553	.648	.703	.741	50	.273	.336	.379	.412
	.684	.753	.793	.821		.354	.410	.449	.479
12	.532	.627	.683	.722	60	.250	.308	.348	.380
	.661	.732	.773	.802		.325	.377	.414	.442
13	.514	.608	.664	.703	70	.232	.286	.324	.354
	.641	.712	.755	.785		.302	.351	.386	.413
14	.497	.590	.646	.686	80	.217	.269	.304	.332
	.623	.694	.737	.768		.283	.330	.362	.389
15	.482	.574	.630	.670	90	.205	.254	.288	.315
	.606	.677	.721	.752		.267	.312	.343	.368
16	.468	.559	.615	.655	100	.195	.241	.274	.300
	.590	.662	.706	.738		.254	.297	.327	.351
17	.456	.545	.601	.641	125	.174	.216	.246	.269
	.575	.647	.691	.724		.228	.266	.294	.316
18	.444	.532	.587	.628	150	.159	.198	.225	.247
	.561	.633	.678	.710		.208	.244	.270	.290
19	.433	.520	.575	.615	200	.138	.172	.196	.215
	.549	.620	.665	.698		.181	.212	.234	.253
20	.423	.509	.563	.604	300	.113	.141	.160	.176
	.537	.608	.652	.685		.148	.174	.192	.208
21	.413	.498	.552	.592	400	.098	.122	.139	.153
	.526	.596	.641	.674		.128	.151	.167	.180
22	.404	.488	.542	.582	500	.088	.109	.124	.137
	.515	.585	.630	.663		.115	.135	.150	.162
23	.396	.479	.532	.572	1000	.062	.077	.088	.097
	.505	.574	.619	.652		.081	.096	.106	.115

SOURCE: Arkin and Colton (1962). *Tables for Statisticians*. Barnes and Noble. Used with permission.
NOTE: Reject the null hypothesis if the *r* value is equal to or greater than that listed in the table.

TABLE F   Random Numbers

30327	18630	50546	66082	41159	13769	69069	98638	78132	89538	76499	07762
64274	43724	09355	95905	69762	61880	27973	33864	58883	27749	24279	96874
52933	23102	68353	73543	39262	95359	15207	34248	72167	78690	44926	10234
99814	52582	88678	52288	06399	89836	39795	25021	89157	10896	80219	31220
10839	96272	18566	71901	05841	86756	83596	72543	00415	93504	28442	99089
64532	28043	50186	97891	46841	47915	60099	46086	51850	98324	03459	88883
79369	56944	72950	96578	23520	59823	18115	19043	77052	05354	16622	13489
72473	18311	07590	41773	74186	76260	77228	41641	25009	67033	75902	08062
06636	31445	70284	28510	58351	79903	38862	66538	81912	62540	33253	36275
14542	14401	59741	18269	68473	00089	56795	89496	71563	25054	37607	32433
97264	30998	86509	05592	27533	73713	36500	31583	70693	16205	60212	98391
48304	13561	61015	55500	34097	95897	47526	60599	80484	67998	75364	89855
44050	25991	24140	98786	59568	69527	77301	35688	12901	95838	13636	75538
61927	12986	56083	58176	96857	76473	55149	48214	57438	04245	04760	82538
67278	02794	59883	81342	25203	74719	58920	62413	64613	28324	75909	05819
51232	71654	62291	86512	38261	68726	80823	44703	61216	40650	86571	31293
76008	18571	70444	50997	41898	97275	45214	75034	93415	79833	30986	25380
53457	92759	15692	40749	20252	94374	32165	85560	72065	91110	91093	43358
02064	42003	29082	66895	46284	60962	81016	42875	39296	73757	47712	59994
96189	93080	72408	50326	21036	67021	66129	05168	72255	46507	40295	82526
60096	18267	88451	20780	13376	86668	37511	77393	45213	54311	41379	46401
92126	74740	62446	49825	03170	07455	80177	07330	82473	86672	14009	91144
27529	41624	97142	03527	40490	82516	26105	23749	90809	85200	76387	71039
28416	05879	41462	72666	13340	46835	82130	89467	59123	49790	06486	10759
88913	26034	01297	81988	63710	52088	28572	78239	69020	17901	05184	21165
67587	21470	75583	30475	79729	82931	83741	80164	87779	20366	96277	69796
26517	06828	85161	01052	56508	65644	68683	40747	70616	74203	76242	32994
43848	96986	41837	47235	28638	73600	29431	03206	18655	22372	93589	53032

SOURCE: Weller and Romney (1988). *Systematic Data Collection.* Sage. Used with permission.

INDEX

ABOUT THE AUTHORS

GENNARO F. VITO is Professor in the School of Justice Administration at the University of Louisville. He received his Ph.D. in public administration from Ohio State University in 1978. He is coauthor of three books: *The American Juvenile Justice System, Probation and Parole in America,* and *Introduction to Criminal Justice Research Methods.* His publications on probation and parole and criminal justice evaluation research have appeared in several journals. He is currently at work on a study of capital sentencing in Kentucky and is the editor of the *American Journal of Criminal Justice.*

EDWARD J. LATESSA is Professor and Head of the Department of Criminal Justice at the University of Cincinnati. He received his Ph.D. in public administration from Ohio State University where he served as Assistant Director of the Program for the Study of Crime and Delinquency. He recently served as Principal Investigator of a national study, "The Impact of Technology in Prisons," funded by the National Institute of Corrections. He is coauthor of two books: *Probation and Parole in America* and *Introduction to Criminal Justice Research Methods.* He has published extensively in the area of corrections and criminal justice. He is also President of the Academy of Criminal Justice Sciences.

NOTES